Growing Old in the Grace of God

Clay Sterrett

Extra copies and a catalog of other materials may be obtained from:
CFC Literature
P.O. Box 245
Staunton, VA 24402-0245
ISBN 0-9760454-5-1
Printed by R. R. Donnelley & Sons, Harrisonburg, VA

DEDICATED TO:

Paul and Christine Knopp
(“Papa” and “Mama”)

A couple who has modeled
for many of us
how to grow older
in the grace of God

‘Tis grace hath brought me safe thus far,
And grace will lead me home.

(John Newton, *Amazing Grace*)

CONTENTS

GROWING OLD IN THE GRACE OF GOD

OBITUARIES
TWO YEARS YOUNGER THAN YOU
TWELVE YEARS OLDER THAN YOU
EXACTLY YOUR AGE
THREE YEARS YOUR JUNIOR
FIVE YEARS YOUR SENIOR
YOUR AGE ON THE DOT

CHAPTER ONE

GROWING OLD IS NOT FOR SISSIES

It is time for this book to be written. This November (2011), I will be celebrating my sixtieth birthday. I can distinctly remember as a teenager thinking that my parents – in their forties – were "old." I can also remember celebrating my fortieth birthday and feeling quite fit and fine. At that point, I thought that the sixties were a time of getting "old." I was thinking that most people I knew in their sixties *looked* old. However, now that I have personally reached this distinguished age of "sixty," I am once again adjusting my thinking because (1) I don't really feel so old and (2) I now know that the *eighties* are when one is really "old." At my current age, I am sobered, by the realization that, statistically speaking, I am likely in the last quarter of my life.

It seems like I am having regular reminders that my life is not "what it used to be." This past year I was sitting in chair of a hair stylist with a black cape wrapped around me. As the lady cut my hair, I noticed the cape was covered with *gray* hair – *my* gray hair! I looked in vain to spot even a small splash of brown hair, but sadly, none was to be found. The gray hair was a strong dose of reality that day. Furthermore, I have faced the fact that I don't have that much hair – regardless of color – to spare anymore!

My whole life I have thoroughly enjoyed the game of basketball. At best I have been a mediocre player, but the heart has always been there and it has been a fun way to get some physical exercise. In recent years I have enjoyed the tee shirt that says, "The Older I Get, the Better I Was." After a (foolish) pick-up game against a few teenagers this year, I thought I had pulled something in both of my knees. The pain was terrible. A doctor told me I was facing a form of arthritis that will inevitably affect every human in the knees or hips if they live long enough. The reality is that I probably need to give up the game. How sad! Am I really *that* old?!

Despite these sobering signs of older age, I feel there is still much life to be lived and "worlds to conquer." Recently, I heard an encouraging quote that "the sixties are the youth of old age." I am going to hold on to that quote for the next ten years!

How You Know You Are Getting Old

These might be some indicators that you are well past your physical prime and are soon to be classified in the not-so-desirable category of "senior citizen."

- You pay close attention to the obituaries.
- You need reading glasses . . .
- . . . then keep forgetting where you put them.
- Everything hurts and what doesn't hurt doesn't work.
- You feel like the morning after, but you haven't been anywhere.
- You get winded playing cards.
- Your children begin to look middle-aged.
- All your friends are looking old.
- Your mind makes contracts your body can't meet.
- You know all the answers, but nobody asks you the questions.
- The rock stars you used to idolize are now potbellied and gray.
- You tell the same story three times to the same person.
- You look forward to a dull evening at home.
- You're turning off the lights for economic reasons, not for romantic reasons.

- You enter a store and totally forget what you came in for.
- Your hair takes less time (or no time) to dry.
- You introduce one of your "best friends" and can't remember his name.
- Getting the mail is one of the highlights of your day.
- Your bathroom visits are much more frequent.
- You tell someone how great she looks, and she doesn't return the compliment.[1]

How is "Old" Defined?

Some dictionary definitions and synonyms would include the following descriptions of "old." The first few seem to be NEGATIVE: (1) advanced in age; not young; (2) decayed shabby, stale; and (3) outdated. Any of those three definitions could leave some of us feeling depressed. However, consider these following descriptions that are POSITIVE: (1) practiced, experienced, and skilled. In Gen. 25:8 it says *Abraham... breathed his last and died at a good old age...* (2) sensible, mature, and wise; and (3) great, plentiful, abundant, and excessive. For example, we might say, "They live in a grand, old house." So, not all definitions of "old" are so bad!

Life Expectancy is Increasing

We often don't realize how blessed we are to live in the 21st century. Consider the following average estimated lifespans in history (keep in mind that the low rate in ancient times is greatly affected by infant mortality).[2]

ERA	AVERAGE LIFESPAN
• Classical Greece/Rome (500 BC – 500 AD)	28 years
• Medieval period (500-1500 AD)	38 years
• Victorian period (1850's –1900)	40 years
• Current world average (est. 2010)	67 years

In our country, largely through vaccines, better living conditions, and improved medical technology, we have seen the average lifespan increase over 20 years in the past century. The U.S. Centers for Disease Control listed the average age for Americans as 77.9 in the year 2007.

The number of older folks is steadily increasing in our country. According to the Pew Research Center, over the next two decades about ten-thousand baby boomers per day will become "seniors" (i.e., sixty-five or older) That is seventy-nine million people! In the U.S., by the year 2030, the older population is expected to include about one in five people.[3]

According to the Bible, any lifespan from "seventy" onward is a long life. Moses wrote, *The length of our days is seventy years – or eighty, if we have the strength...*[4] King David died at seventy years of age, described as *a good old age.*[5] The Bible has multiple promises for old age, such as, *Even in old age they will still produce fruit; they will remain vital and green.*[6] Christians in every stage of life ought to be optimistic; for the believer – no matter what the age – the best is yet to come! *No eye has seen, no ear has heard, no mind has conceived what God has prepared for those who love him.*[7] Poet Robert Browning expressed this idea well.

> Grow old along with me!
> The best is yet to be,
> The last of life, for which the first was made.[8]

E. Stanley Jones wrote, "Old age is just a new page upon which you can write life's noblest chapter."[9] This book is intended to present a very optimistic view of our latter years. We will address some hard issues, but will encourage an eternal and positive perspective. Without strong faith motivating us in the present and a hope anticipating a great future, we will surely retreat into a sense of foreboding and anxiety about our aging. This is why it has been said, "Growing old is not for sissies!" I know I am currently being challenged to live out my days by the grace of God, for the glory of God. I will not buy into the "retirement mentality." Like Jones, I want to "write life's noblest chapter."

CHAPTER TWO

KEEPING AN ETERNAL PERSPECTIVE

> *Therefore we do not lose heart. Though outwardly we are wasting away, yet inwardly we are being renewed day by day. For our light and momentary troubles are achieving for us an eternal glory that far outweighs them all. So we fix our eyes not on what is seen, but on what is unseen. For what is seen is temporary, but what is unseen is eternal. (2 Cor.4:16-18)*

Richard Baxter, an English Puritan leader in the seventeenth century, was chronically ill and had plenty of reason to be a miserable man during his lifetime. Tubercular from his teens, Baxter suffered constantly from indigestion, kidney stones, headaches, toothaches, swollen limbs, internal bleeding. He endured all this before the days of pain-relieving drugs. In spite of his physical condition, Baxter was outgoing, energetic, and uncomplaining. By 1661, he had evangelized his entire town of Kidderminster, which had a population of two thousand adults, plus children. Baxter also wrote regularly, producing some classic devotional books which are still used by many Christians. In one of these books, *The Saint's Everlasting Rest*, he tells his secret. From his thirtieth year, he practiced a habit which he began when he thought he was about to die: for about a half-an-hour each day Baxter would meditate on the life to come and the glories awaiting him. This practice instilled hope in his heart and gave this radiant servant of Christ the motivation and strength to persevere. Having an eternal perspective made the difference in the life of Richard Baxter, and it can make a difference in our lives as well.

Facing Some Unpleasant Realities

It is a sobering Scripture passage that states, *outwardly we are wasting away.*[1] It could be quite depressing if all we have to live for is this present world. I can remember my mom, just before she died in her eighties, looking at her sagging skin on her arms with multiple dark bruises and expressing her sadness in watching herself physically deteriorating. Yet, she also had a great hope in the resurrection of Christ and she looked forward to being renewed in body and spirit. *For when the trumpet sounds, the Christians who have died will be raised with transformed bodies. And then we who are living will be transformed so that we will never die. For our perishable earthly bodies must be transformed into heavenly bodies that will never die.*[2]

The book of Ecclesiastes exhorts us *to remember your Creator in the days of your youth...*[3] Why? Because the older we get, the more we decline physically and mentally. This description from the book can be rather depressing.

> *And when your teeth are gone, keep your lips tightly closed when you eat! Even the chirping of birds will wake you up. But you yourself will be deaf and tuneless, with a quavering voice. You will be afraid of heights and of falling, white-haired and withered, dragging along without any sexual desire. You will be standing at death's door. And as you near your everlasting home, the mourners will walk along the streets. Yes, remember your Creator now while you are young, before the silver cord of life snaps and the golden bowl is broken. Don't wait until the water jar is smashed at the spring and the pulley is broken at the well. For then the dust will return to the earth, and the spirit will return to God who gave it.*[4]

As we grow older we may face any number of new challenges. The following are some symptoms of those over sixty-five years of age.[5]

- Approximately 40% have some hearing loss.
- One woman in four suffers from osteoporosis, the bone-thinning disease.
- An estimated 50% have some arthritis or joint pain.
- Increased skin wrinkles are to be expected.
- About half have some evidence of heart disease.
- The lenses in our eyes become more opaque and many develop cataracts, which can be treated successfully if detected early.
- Chronic constipation is a common complaint.

We don't like to think much about these realities of our temporal life as we grow older and there are a thousand ways we try to avoid them. But, the world's media constantly shouts at us, "Live for yourself! Now is the time! Enjoy yourself! After all, you deserve it!" If we buy into this temporal mentality, our priorities really become twisted, as Mark Buchanan explained.

> The world turns this inside out and backward. Many of us attempt, often desperately and at great cost, to be outwardly renewed day by day, while inwardly we waste away. We pour out time and money and energy to look beautiful, to have pleasure, to feel good about ourselves, to avoid suffering. Every year we spend billions of dollars on diets and gyms and cosmetics and surgeries and prescriptions and leisure crafts and getaways – all in a vain attempt to reverse our

> outward wasting. Yet the wasting relentlessly presses on, blithely and cruelly indifferent to our defenses. All the while, we wither on the inside, lonely, empty, afraid.[6]

There are multiple things that could seem unpleasant about old age, especially declining health and the loss of a mate, parents, or siblings. Our perspective will make quite a difference as we experience such things. Will we just look at things *outwardly* and sink into depression and despair? The twofold remedy is found in our introductory Scripture: (1) We must allow our inner man to be renewed. This primarily occurs from Scripture reading and meditation.[7] (2) We *fix our eyes on what is unseen;* in other words, we make a conscious effort to look at life with an *eternal* perspective. Jonathan Edwards is quoted as saying, "Lord, stamp eternity on my eyeballs."

A Psalm About Eternity – Psalm 90

There is one portion of Scripture that especially encourages an eternal perspective – Psalm 90. This psalm is traditionally believed to have been written by Moses at the end of the desert wanderings. Some scholars believe it is the oldest piece of writing in the Bible next to the book of Job. Here is a portion of the psalm.

> *Lord, you have been our dwelling place*
> *throughout all generations.*
> *Before the mountains were born*
> *or you brought forth the earth and the world,*
> *from everlasting to everlasting you are God....*
> *All our days pass away under your wrath;*
> *we finish our years with a moan.*
> *The length of our days is seventy years –*
> *or eighty, if we have the strength;*
> *yet their span is but trouble and sorrow,*
> *for they quickly pass, and we fly away.*

Who knows the power of your anger?
For your wrath is as great as the fear that is due you.
Teach us to number our days aright,
that we may gain a heart of wisdom.[8]

There are several important points in this psalm.

1. **God is an eternal God.**

When we speak of "eternal life," it does not just mean that we are going to live for a long time; it means a higher *quality* of life that is uniquely found in God. When Jesus said, *"I have come to give you life in all its fullness,"*[9] it means life different from anything we have ever naturally experienced.

Will we continue "for ever and ever" in our present natural life, or will we live in a dimension of supernatural life? Will we live as citizens of the Kingdom of God? *In him was life, and that life was the light of men.*[10] *He who has the Son has life; he who does not have the Son of God does not have life.*[11] Right now we can begin to experience a God-dimension of life, and this will continue on and on. C.S. Lewis commented on this theme.

> Christianity asserts that every individual human being is going to live for ever, and this must be either true or false. Now there are a good many things which would not be worth bothering about if I were going to live only seventy years, but which I had better bother about very seriously if I am going to live for ever. Perhaps my bad temper or my jealousy are gradually getting worse – so gradually that the increase in seventy years will not be very noticeable. But it might be absolute hell in a million years: in fact, if Christianity is true, Hell is the precisely correct technical term for what it would be.[12]

I have noticed that older people, unless there is some disease that affects their brain, often magnify qualities of life that have either been good or bad. In other words, a person who has been a constant complainer and critic will only become a worse critic the older he gets. If a person lives in bitterness, that bitterness will be amplified. In contrast, a man with a sweet, joyful spirit, will manifest that same joy and sweetness – even great joy – at the very end. Dawson Trotman said it succinctly, "You are going to be what you are now becoming."[13]

2. **Life is short.**

Psalm 90 describes our life in several expressions:

...like *a passing day.* (v. 4a)
...like *a watch in the night.* (v. 4b)
...like *grass which can quickly wither.* (vv. 5-6)
...like *a sigh.* (v. 9)
...like years which *quickly pass.* (v. 10)

For many years I have taught eleventh grade students on the subject of Bible ethics. In a recent class we were discussing some issues involving dating and relationships and one student said, "Mr. Sterrett, you need to realize we are only one third your age..." I wasn't immediately offended or intimidated; I thought my words were still relevant! But, it did cause me to reflect.

Then, last year I attended a high school reunion – my fortieth reunion! During that weekend event, I noticed how old many of my contemporaries looked (and maybe they were observing the same thing about me). I just couldn't get away from the stark reality – it was FORTY YEARS AGO that I was in high school! Yet, in many ways, it did not seem that long ago. Time does fly, doesn't it?

3. **Eternity can motivate us to greater godliness.**

Betty Malz, during a time of near death on a hospital bed, had an "out-of-body experience" and afterwards wrote a best selling book, *My Glimpse of Eternity.*[14] Her experience radically changed her life – especially increasing her love for people, regardless of their race or social background. Those who catch any glimpse of eternity are usually strongly motivated to live godly lives. There are some excellent prayers in Psalm 90 that we can make our own.

PRAYER #1

Teach us to number our days. (v. 12)

One thing most time-management courses miss is the fear of God as a motivator. One must have a *sense of eternity* before he will likely use time wisely for the glory of God. James Dobson wrote,

> If we really grasped the numbering of our days as Moses wrote in the 90th Psalm, we would surely be motivated to invest ourselves primarily in eternal values....Would men and women devote their lives to the pursuit of wealth and status symbols if they realized how soon their possessions would be torn from their trembling hands? It is the illusion of permanence, you see, that distorts our perception and shapes our selfish behavior. When eternal values come in view, it becomes our greatest desire to please our Lord and influence as many others for Him as possible...[15]

As we consider the days we have remaining on this earth, what will we seek after – financial security? Resting in a life of retirement? Or, taking that long-awaited vacation? A famous quote that we probably heard from grandparents stated, "If you have your health, you have everything." Is that so? We can have good health and prosperity, and yet miss out on eternal life.[16] None of the good things in life are bad in themselves, but where does the Lord fit in? Are we *seeking first* the Kingdom of God?[17] Are we using any of our latter time and energy to serve the Lord? I love this poem by Frances Havergal.

Ask your King to take you wholly into His service,
and place all the hours of this day quite simply
at His disposal, and ask Him to make and keep you
ready to do just exactly what He appoints.
Never mind about tomorrow; one day at a time is
enough.[18]

PRAYER #2

Make us glad for as many days as you have afflicted us.(v. 15)

The *New Living Translation* says, "*Give us gladness in proportion to our former misery!*" The *Jerusalem Bible* says, "*Make our future as happy as our past was sad.*" A view of eternity can help us endure the miseries of this present life.

> A pagan, Andrianus by name, deeply impressed by the fortitude of the persecuted Christians, asked, "What is it which makes these Christians bear these sufferings?" "The unseen things of heaven," was the reply. This was the secret of the radiant and persevering martyrs.[19]

Some of us may have to endure severe physical pain in this life. Some of us might suffer disappointments in a mate or heartaches about a child. No matter what hardship or disappointment comes our way, we can realize along with Scottish hymn writer, Horatius Bonar, that "One hour of eternity, one moment with the Lord, will make us utterly forget a lifetime of desolations."[20]

PRAYER #3

Let the favor of the Lord our God rest upon us, and establish the work of our hands upon us, yes, establish the work of our hands! (v. 17 ESV)

Just about anybody who serves the Lord wants their work to have eternal consequences. One of the great motivators in my life is found in this passage.

> *By the grace God has given me, I laid a foundation as an expert builder, and someone else is building on it. But each one should be careful how he builds. For no one can lay any foundation other than the one already laid, which is Jesus Christ. If any man builds on this foundation using gold, silver, costly stones, wood, hay or straw, his work will be shown for what it is, because the Day will bring it to light. It will be revealed with fire, and the fire will test the quality of each man's work. If what he has built survives, he will receive his reward.* [21]

Wood, hay and straw come in abundant quantities and are easily found. Gold, silver, and precious stones, on the other hand, are quite rare and hard to find. It is a sobering thing to realize that probably the majority of religious works will be burned up at the judgment seat of Christ. Therefore, I have a great desire to be involved only in works that will be more like *gold, silver, and precious stones* – works that are built on the foundation of Jesus, that will withstand the fire of the Master, and have lasting fruit – affecting people for eternity.

After turning fifty, I have had multiple invitations to teach seminars to Christian leaders in both India and Uganda. At age sixty, I could begin to rationalize that I ought to slow down, but each year the Holy Spirit nudges me onward. I feel a strong compulsion to "work while it is day." I believe my most valuable years of ministry in life may very well be those in the next twenty years (if the Lord so wills).

In closing this section, I will share a poem from a ninety-year-old believer, Ernest Barkaway. This friend of Joni Eareckson Tada's had the right perspective about viewing all of life in light of eternity.

They say that I am growing old;
I've heard them say times untold,
In language plain and bold –
But I am not growing old.
This frail old shell in which I dwell is growing old,
I know full well!
But I am not the shell.
What if my hair is turning gray?
Gray hairs are honorable they say.
What if my eyesight's growing dim?
I still can see to follow Him
Who sacrificed His life for me –
Upon the Cross at Calvary!
Why should I care if time's old plough
Has left its furrows on my brow?
Another house, not made with hands
Awaits me in the Glory Land.
What though I falter in my walk
And though my tongue refuse to talk?
I still can tread the narrow way;
I still can watch and pray!
The robe of flesh I'll drop and rise
To seize the everlasting prize.
I'll meet you on the streets of gold
And prove I am NOT growing old.[22]

CHAPTER THREE

BATTLING THE BEAUTY MYTH

This chapter will definitely be more applicable to ladies than men for a very simple reason – older men generally don't seem to be too concerned about deteriorating or out-of-shape bodies, but for many women – IT IS A BIG DEAL!

Here are three revealing questions that I have often asked a class of teenagers.

- How many of you ladies, if you were to *compare* yourselves to most other ladies your age, would feel that you are not very beautiful?
- How many of you ladies, if you could suddenly be *transformed* into the most beautiful girl on the east coast, would choose to be so changed? (And, if you could, why would men be attracted to you?)
- How many of you (both men and ladies), if you could, would *change* something about your physical body?

The answers to these questions will likely demonstrate how we are influenced most about the way we view ourselves – are we influenced more by vanity, the world's media, or by the Bible?

Some Interesting Statistics[1]

- % of women who say they would change something about their looks if they could – 99%

- % of men who say they would change something about their looks if they could – 94%

- Average score Americans give themselves on a scale of one to ten, on their looks – 6.5

- Women especially seem to have negative thoughts about themselves....While only one man in ten is "strongly dissatisfied" with his body, one third of women are "strongly dissatisfied" with theirs. Though both sexes are overweight in equal proportions (about one-third), 95% of enrollees in weight loss programs are women.

- In a *Glamour* survey of 33,000 women, 75% of those aged 18 to 35 believed they were too fat, while only 25% were medically overweight. In addition, 45% of the *underweight* women thought they were too fat.

- It is estimated that 5 to 10% of all American girls and women have anorexia. Each year it is estimated that 150,000 American women die of anorexia....this problem has especially been prevalent in our present generation. A generation ago, the average model weighed 8% less than the average American woman, whereas today she weighs 23% less....

- This affects children as well. In a survey of 494 middle-class schoolgirls in San Francisco, more than one-half described themselves as overweight, while only 15% were so by medical standards. Thirty-one percent of nine-year-olds thought they were too fat, and 81 % of the ten-year-olds were dieters.

- Anywhere from 200,000 to 1 million American women have had their breasts cut open and sacs of chemical gel implanted. In a 1986 Psychology Today survey, one-third of American women were unhappy with the size or shape of their breasts.

- In the 1989 Miss America pageant, at least five contestants were surgically reconstructed by the same Arkansas plastic surgeon.

- Cosmetic surgery denies reality. Cosmetic surgery is not "cosmetic" and human flesh is not "plastic".... Instead of surgery, doctors use expressions like "a tummy tuck."

- Liposuction is now one of the most popular of cosmetic surgeries...in which a tube is inserted and sucks out portions of tissue, fat, and nerves. 198,000 American women underwent the procedure in 2009.

- The top five surgical procedures in 2009, according to the American Society of Plastic Surgeons, were:
    1. Breast augmentation – 289,000
    2. Nose reshaping – 256,000
    3. Eyelid surgery – 203,000
    4. Liposuction – 198,00
    5. Tummy tuck – 115,000

- Cosmetic surgeries increased to over 12 million in 2009, almost ten times the number 20 years ago! Of these 12 million patients, 91% were women.

- There were 4,795,357 Botox procedures in 2009 (94% were women patients).

- Americans spent over $10 billion on cosmetic surgery in 2009.

What do you think is a root reason for such an increase in these statistics in recent times? Certainly media influence is a factor, but even more, we are increasingly becoming a self-centered society, as Scripture has described. *But mark this: There will be terrible times in the last days. People will be lovers of themselves...lovers of pleasure rather than lovers of God.*[2]

This is why it is crucial, especially the older we get, to consider…

God's Perspective On Beauty

1. **Many women in the Bible are described as "beautiful."**

God is certainly not against beauty; he created a world full of beauty![3] In the Bible, some ladies are specifically called "beautiful" or "lovely."

- Sarah – Her husband said, *"I know what a beautiful woman you are."*[4]
- Rebekah – *The girl was very beautiful...*[5]
- Rachel – *Rachel was lovely in form, and beautiful.*[6]
- Esther – *This girl...was lovely in form and features…*[7]
- Abigail – *She was an intelligent and beautiful woman...*[8]

Abigail represents a good combination – she was both *intelligent* and *beautiful.* When the Bible uses the word, *intelligent*, it does not necessarily mean high mental capacity; it means someone who has good sense and understanding; someone who is also prudent – who carefully makes wise decisions with the future in mind.[9] An *intelligent* person seeks after true knowledge. I have always appreciated elderly people who still love the word of God and read it daily. Many a time when I would visit one man in his nineties, I would find him sitting in his rocking chair beside a wood stove, grinning as he read the Bible, and ready to share some nugget of truth that he was discovering that morning.

2. **The Hebrew word for "beautiful" implies both an external and internal beauty.**

Two Hebrew words used for *beautiful* give these definitions: that which is good to the senses, fair, pleasant, and desirable; that which is morally good, honest, becoming, and virtuous; that which is right – as a thing ought to be. The word is used in the creation account: *And God saw that is was good*.[10] The words *beautiful* and *good* are synonymous.[11]

I can remember seeing a film about the last days of Corrie ten Boom. At the end of the film, it showed a successive number of photos of her face, one after another. Although she was quite elderly, and there was no "movie star" beauty about her, as I looked in her eyes, I began to weep, as I could see the eyes of Jesus. Even in the midst of frail humanity, there was an internal beauty shining forth.

CORRIE TEN BOOM

On the other hand, at times I have seen famous movie stars interviewed who are gorgeous outwardly, but are very shallow in their conversations. It is rare to see an inner beauty shining forth from their eyes. The eyes of a person are quite telling; the Bible says, *Your eyes are like a window for your body.*[12]

Scripture warns against a life that is only concerned about outward appearance.

> *...You hypocrites! You are like whitewashed tombs, which look beautiful on the outside but on the inside are filled of dead men's bones and everything unclean.*[13]

> *Don't be concerned about the outward beauty that depends on fancy hairstyles, expensive jewelry, or beautiful clothes. You should be known for the beauty that comes from within, the unfading beauty of a gentle and quiet spirit, which is so precious to God. That is the way the holy women of old made themselves beautiful...*[14]

The Bible is not against using jewelry or make-up. A legalistic lady asked a country preacher one day, "Preacher, do you believe Christians should use make-up?" He responded, "Well, if my barn needs painting, I paint it!" There can be a legitimate place for fixing ourselves up. The passage above seems to warn against those who are *only* concerned or *excessively* concerned about their external appearance, to the neglect of their inner beauty.

3. Beauty can be deceitful.

> *Charm is deceptive and beauty is fleeting; but a woman who fears the Lord is to be praised.*[15]

I once saw a photo of some former actresses who had been sexy stars in older James Bond movies – movies that were extremely popular when I was a young man. These six ladies were now at least in their seventies, and needless to say, some of the "glory had faded!" It is a stark fact of life that many will try their best to avoid: no matter how attractive a woman might be, the time will come when any objective person will have to admit that the outward beauty is *fleeting*.

The verse above says, *Charm is deceptive.* Why is this so? The answer is simply because beauty is *not lasting.* The physical bodies of everyone – without exception – *are* going to wear out. We are mortal; we are in a process of decay; we will one day return to dust.

Some folks are quite fearful and simply obsessed with themselves. I can remember seeing Michael Jackson, as he was closing in on fifty years of age, being so paranoid, spending time regularly in an oxygen tank, saying he wanted to live to be two-hundred! When celebrities (or any of us) fail to emphasize more the inner beauty that only comes through Christ, they will likely live a life of vanity.

4. **Beauty can lead to a fall.**

There are often more disadvantages to being beautiful than not being so beautiful. Some of the most physically attractive people are not only very unhappy, but they often doubt their attractiveness. Interviews with Miss America pageant winners often reveal they dislike several physical characteristics about their bodies.

The media does not always portray reality – because the majority of the actors are very good looking, of course with quite a bit of make-up help. In reality, most people are pretty ordinary looking. At times when I am sitting in international airports, I like to just watch people, from all kinds of backgrounds and nationalities. Although occasionally a very attractive person will walk by, it strikes me that most people are *not* attractive; they are just ordinary looking. Abe Lincoln once remarked, "Common people are the best in the world; that is the reason the Lord made so many of them."[16]

There can actually be some *disadvantages* of being extremely beautiful. Many men might be attracted to a very beautiful woman – but primarily for physical interests.

Why were so many people drawn to Jesus? Was it because of his physical appearance? The Bible says, *He had no beauty or majesty to attract us to him, nothing in his appearance that we should desire him.*[17]

In the Bible we see that beauty can also lead to a fall. In one passage talking about the vanity of the king of Tyre, we also see an allusion to Satan – a description of one who was once a glorious archangel in heaven, *You were the model of perfection, full of wisdom and perfect in beauty.*[18] Apparently, Satan became infatuated with his own beauty, and it led to his rebellion and eventual expulsion from heaven. *Your heart became proud on account of your beauty, and you corrupted your wisdom because of your splendor. So I threw you to the earth; I made a spectacle of you before kings.*[19]

If we are endowed with physical beauty, we can give thanks to God. If we are *not* endowed with physical beauty, we can still give thanks to God. We are *all* "fearfully and wonderfully made."

5. **Our heart affects our face**.

The Bible says, *A happy heart makes the face cheerful.*[20] What's inside us reflects what's outside. For example, a person with a grumpy attitude will often display a grumpy face. I remember meeting an elderly lady at a nursing home. It soon became apparent she had a lot of racial hatred in her heart. "I hate black people!" she said as she clenched her arthritic fingers. The more she talked, the more twisted her body became. In her case, I believe her outward afflictions were a direct result of her inward hatred.

On the other side, I remember meeting a dear lady who was dying of cancer in a Manchester, New Hampshire, hospital. People had anointed her with oil and prayed for healing, but she had not been healed and knew she would soon leave behind her husband and children. Her body was wasting away, her hair was gone, and she had difficulty talking for long. Yet, those who went inside her room became acutely aware of a most beautiful woman, in love with her Lord, and ready to soon depart from this earth and meet Him face-to-face. She had a sweet smile and such a lovely countenance on her face. It was like something of heaven was radiating through her feeble body. Any who visited her (including me) to bring encouragement came away as the ones who had been encouraged! She remained in this state until she died a week later.

6. **We can learn to accept those physical characteristics we cannot change**.

There are some defects about ourselves we can and should change. A lady I was acquainted with only had two crooked front teeth, and when she grinned one couldn't help but notice. Someone helped her financially, and one day she showed up with a mouth full of brand new (false) teeth! She looked so much better, and people were not distracted as they talked with her.

What defects should be corrected? Bill Gothard once said we ought to consider changing anything that might be a distraction from our words – especially messages God wants to communicate through us.[21]

What about physical changes we can't change – e.g., our height, color of eyes, our build, color of skin, even our basic intellectual abilities? There are three biblical truths to keep in mind.

- When we *compare* ourselves with others *we are not wise.* (II Cor. 10:12)
- We are not a piece of junk; we *are God's work of art...* (Eph. 2:10)
- We are *fearfully and wonderfully made...* Before creation, God designed the particular parts of our body – for his glory! (Ps. 139:13-16)

Therefore, even when we are troubled by a physical defect, we can praise God for our bodies.

In 1820, a six-week-old girl was given the wrong medication for her eyes. As a result, she became permanently blind. Instead of becoming bitter in life, she responded to the training of her faithful grandmother. Soon she memorized verses, then chapters, and finally could quote entire books of the Bible.

When she was eight years old, she wrote her first poem,

O what a happy soul am I
    Although I cannot see;
I am resolved that in this world
    Contented I will be.
How many blessings I enjoy
    That other people don't.
To weep and sigh because I'm blind
    I cannot and I won't.

Her writing continued until, by the age of eighty-six, eight to nine thousand hymns and gospel songs had flowed from her dedicated life. Her spirit and mind were so keenly developed that she could compose up to fifteen songs simultaneously.

Her life and writings have strengthened the lives of countless people. When she would give her testimony in meetings, her listeners would sit in awe as she lifted their spiritual eyes into the presence of her Savior. Perhaps more people have come to salvation by her songs than by any other music.

She was the first woman ever to speak from the floor of the Senate in Washington, D.C.

Songs like "Blessed Assurance," and "All the Way My Savior Leads Me," and thousands of others are loved and sung by millions of people today.

Her name is Francis Jane Crosby, better known to us as Fanny Crosby.[22]

7. **Believers can be optimistic – one day we will have renewed, imperishable bodies.**

Probably the most encouraging passage in the Bible for handicapped or elderly folks whose bodies are wearing out is found in I Corinthians 15 – the "resurrection chapter." May it encourage our hearts today!

> *It is the same way for the resurrection of the dead. Our earthly bodies, which die and decay, will be different when they are resurrected, for they will never die. Our bodies now disappoint us, but when they are raised, they will be full of glory. They are weak now, but when they are raised, they will be full of power. They are natural human bodies now, but when they are raised, they will be spiritual bodies. For just as there are natural bodies, so also there are spiritual bodies.... Every human being has an earthly body just like Adam's, but our heavenly bodies will be just like Christ's....What I am saying, dear brothers and sisters, is that flesh and blood cannot inherit the Kingdom of God. These perishable bodies of ours are not able to live forever. But let me tell you a wonderful secret God has revealed to us. Not all of us will die, but we will all be transformed. It will happen in a moment, in the blinking of an eye, when the last trumpet is blown. For when the trumpet sounds, the Christians who have died will be raised with transformed bodies. And then we who are living will be transformed so that we will never die. For our perishable earthly bodies must be transformed into heavenly bodies that will never die.*[23]

So, Let's Give Thanks To God

Please join your heart with this verbal expression of thanksgiving.

Thank you, Heavenly Father, for creating my body
in your own special way.
I thank you I am wonderfully made.
I thank you even for features I have wanted to change.
Help me not to compare my body and mind to others.
Create in me an inner beauty that will last forever.
Grant me a cheerful heart that will affect my entire
countenance, and reflect Christ's love to others.
In Christ's name, Amen.

CHAPTER FOUR

CLEANING OUT THE CLUTTER

In preparing this chapter, I consulted various dictionaries for definitions of the word "clutter." Here are a few:

- A disorderly assemblage
- A confused collection
- A crowded disorder
- An untidy state
- Litter; scattered rubbish

There is now a television show about people who are *hoarders*. Their homes are so full of clutter there is nowhere to sit down; there is no empty table or shelf space to set anything; and there is no sense of orderliness.

God is a God of order.[1] When God created the universe, it was no haphazardly accomplished task. We can look at the mighty stars or a tiny butterfly and see the handiwork of a Creator God who desires for *all things to be done properly [beautifully and gracefully] and in an orderly manner [according to proper arrangement].*[2]

Before going any further, let me emphasize that we can certainly go through life being very disorganized and haphazard and still experience the blessing of God on our lives. God's grace is certainly not restricted to how neat and orderly we are! Some of the neatest persons may be far from God and some of the dearest and deepest believers may not be very organized in their personal affairs. We must agree that God is first and foremost interested in the matters of the *heart.*

It is my persuasion, however, that God can accomplish much more through our finite lives if they are in good order and free of clutter. In writing to the Colossian church, Paul said he rejoiced in seeing two qualities in their lives: *For though I am absent in body, yet I am with you in spirit, rejoicing to see your good order and the firmness of your faith in Christ.*[3] The word *order* in the above verse is a military word that means "a good arrangement, an orderly condition."[4]

Getting organized and cleaning out the clutter can be beneficial, and it will be a true service of love to those who will eventually handle our estate after death. It is best to make such deliberate plans while we are still physically capable and mentally sharp.

Before We Turn Seventy...

We ought to seriously consider some practical steps like...

- Organizing and simplifying our paperwork
- Getting our finances and will in good order
- Distributing some possessions
- Downsizing our property
- Cleaning out the clutter!

This chapter will examine each of these practical steps that will be difficult for those who are by nature pack-rats or those who lived through the Great Depression (these folks usually don't like to throw *anything* away.) However, if we can resolve to clean out the clutter, it ought to make things simpler for us in the days ahead.

Organize and Simplify Our Paperwork

In the homes of many older folks, there is often a lot of worthless paperwork lying around. This may include old newspapers and magazines that will likely *not* be read again, junk mail, bills, outdated phone books or catalogs, old cards that have some sentimental attachment, and important papers that might easily get lost in all the clutter.

I personally deal with a considerable amount of paperwork between personal mail, e-mails, magazines, papers, as well as a lot of printed material from our church (since I am a pastor). I have adopted a helpful procedure that I now will pass on to you.

WHEN YOU ACQUIRE A PIECE OF PAPER

1. Discard it if it is obviously "junk mail." (Don't even waste time in opening such items.)
2. Stack it (in a file or stack tray) if it needs correspondence or careful reading.
3. File it away – if it is important – like receipts, tax info, financial reports.

When I receive mail, I go through junk mail first, quickly discarding anything that I am not interested in or that will be a waste of time for me even to open. That usually leaves me with only a few pieces – bills to pay or relevant correspondence. The bills go in one tray, and in another stack I keep books, magazines, and newsletters to be read; however, I don't let this stack get too big before I set aside time to go through it.

Almost everyone would benefit from using a simple file drawer or box with a set of labeled hanging files. Such files might include:

- Copy of will/ important papers
- Last year's tax forms (file older ones in a separate box)
- This year's taxes (receipts, etc.)
- Health insurance
- Health info – personal records
- Car insurance and title
- Life insurance
- Financial records/ credit cards

- Bank statements (recent; file older ones away in a separate box)
- Family info
- Upcoming trips
- Visa/MC receipts

In addition, when a particular file is overflowing with paperwork (like old receipts, taxes, etc.) the excess can be filed in some storage boxes.

If you feel incapable of such organization, ask a person who is gifted in organizing to assist you in becoming initially established. I have sometimes taken a day or two and helped a person set up files and organize paperwork. It makes it much simpler for them after they see how it's done. There are also individuals who have a business that specializes in assisting older people – who have no family or friends to help – getting organized and downsizing when necessary.[5]

Simplify Our Possessions

When I helped clean out the clothes of one deceased relative, I counted ninety-five shirts! Amazing! I know this man probably never wore more than a dozen of these shirts, but I guess he thought they were all "too good to throw away." I would encourage every person over age fifty to start taking one room at a time and asking a few basic questions:

- Have I used this item anytime in the past five years?
- If it's broken, why am I keeping it?
- Do I really think my grandchildren will want this old item? (They usually want new stuff!)
- Even if it's worth a dollar, is it worth my trouble trying to get the dollar for it?

I am thankful that my wife is not a pack-rat, and we usually work well together in going through old items.

Sometimes, when we clean out a room, we donate anything in good shape to local charities such as Goodwill, Salvation Army, or Valley Rescue Mission.

On occasions we have yard sales. Even though they can be a lot of hassle, the end result is usually worth it. At the end of a yard sale, we usually bring nothing back into the house. We separate anything remaining into two piles – one for local charities and the other for the trash.

Get Our Finances and Will in Good Order

We must occasionally ask ourselves – if I was to die today, would any family members know where my banking accounts, investments, and will are located? Do I even have a will and if so, is my will up-to-date? Do I have all my investments listed on one document? Are my different accounts organized in such a way that family members could understand clearly? Would they understand the "big picture?"

When one of my aunts died, I was the executor of her estate, and it was a mess! I had to sort through files and piece together from scratch the "big picture." In the back of one file I found a crumpled up page – which represented a few thousand dollars of stock! In addition, some other stocks should have been sold in previous years, but my elderly aunt just ignored some of her investments.

In organizing any kind of paperwork, sometimes we need to set aside an extended time – maybe even a couple days – to clean out clutter, organize, and make lists. And, these lists ought to be in a place easily found, or copies given to adult children.

It was said that Franklin D. Roosevelt made extensive notes about having a very simple funeral, instead of a lot of fanfare. After a very elaborate public funeral, his paper was discovered – too late to implement his simple wishes! So, make sure any will or important papers can easily be found, that duplicate copies are in two locations (in case of fire), and that at least two family members know where the papers are located (or have their own sealed copies).

Before my mother died, she downsized her possessions in preparation for moving to a retirement home. She made lists of certain items to give my four brothers and me that she thought might interest us. This early distribution made dividing up her remaining possessions much easier after her death.

If you own old furniture, jewelry, or valuable items, does anyone know their significance? A ring might have been your grandmother's wedding ring, but will anyone know? A necklace may casually be given away that would have some sentimental value as a family heirloom. A set of dishes may be quite valuable, but sold cheaply at a yard sale. While in our sound minds, we should take the time to make inventory lists and document any future intentions.

Downsize Our Property

This is the difficult one for many parents! Often "the old home place" carries such sentimental attachments, it may be difficult to sell, even though it is way too big for one or two people and desperately needs updating to be a sufficient dwelling. This residential dilemma does not usually have a simple solution. In some cases, it works out best for elderly parents to live out their days in the only place they will ever consider to be "home."

After my father died, my mother was left alone in a good-sized house all alone. After a year or so, she realized she needed to make a change, yet she wanted to be close to my family. She offered to sell us the house, which she realized would be a good provision for our family with young children and also a place we would use for church-related fellowship. We estimated converting part of the house into an apartment for her, which would also have a walkway into our house. It proved more economical to buy a small house just up the street from us. She enjoyed living on one smaller floor plan, had a much smaller yard, and had easy access to our family whenever she needed help.

Even while writing this book, we are in the process of assisting my mother-in-law in downsizing from a large home she has lived in for over fifty years to a two bedroom townhouse, with one-level living and no yard to maintain. She is excited about the change, and already it has proved to be a good move for her.

Downsizing is a decision we ought to make while we are still mentally sharp. The older we get, the less likely we are to make such a hard decision, and then we will no longer physically be able to care for the house as we once did. It will tend to deteriorate, and we will either have to frequently ask family members to help or pay workers to maintain it. As we get older, we must seriously consider if downsizing would ultimately make life easier for us (and eventually our children).

Clean Out the Clutter

As I stated in the beginning of this chapter, before we turn seventy, we ought to give serious consideration to *cleaning out the clutter!* Get help from a younger friend or relative if you need to. You will likely need some help to pack and move items. You can take your time, but deliberately go through your house, room by room, and set aside anything that is no longer useful and only taking up space. We may try to justify our clutter by saying we'll "maybe use it someday," but deep inside we know that we never will! Many things can simply be thrown away. Some things can go to local charities, and some can be distributed to family members now – instead of after your death. Here are some things in particular you might check, in addition to what I have already suggested.

1. Get rid of old magazines and out-of-date catalogs.
2. Get rid of old phone books. Make an updated list of most often called numbers. Keep a copy at each phone.

3. Sort through the kitchen "catch all" basket or box. Probably three-fourths of this stuff can be tossed.
4. Go through your recipe box. Only keep your favorites.
5. Sort through photos. My wife, Teresa, and I realized that if we both died, our two sons would only be interested in a small portion of our photos. So, we took a couple days in the winter months and went through over a dozen photo albums and other boxes of photos. Some of these were labeled to clarify names or dates. We made two albums for each of our two sons, kept a group of photos in a box for just us to enjoy, and as hard as it was – tossed out many old family photos.
6. Simplify family history. What old photos and artifacts of former generations will our sons and daughters be interested in? I once helped my mother go through a lot of old photos, and we made five scrapbooks for my brothers and me of grandparents going back to four generations on both sides. The books included the photos, names, and dates of their lifespan.
7. Sort through all the old projects and papers from children. We realized, after our two sons left home, that one day they probably would *not* want all their old report cards, school art projects, sports trophies, baby clothes, etc. So we made a box for each, with special selected items they may one day enjoy having.
8. Review all the framed photos. Do some need to be put away in your new scrapbooks? Can some be tossed? Do some need updated frames?
9. Why keep all your old yearbooks? I kept one high school (my senior year) and one college. I have never missed the ones I tossed.
10. Throw out old letters, cards, and stationary. Maybe save just a few special ones.
11. Throw out old books, novels, or cookbooks. If good enough, some may be donated to the public library.
12. Are there old cassettes, records, CD's, or movies you need to eliminate? I have thrown out almost all my cassettes. Some movies can be donated to the library.

13. Any food that is past expiration dates. Does the freezer need cleaning out?
14. Clothes that no longer fit or that you *never* wear.
15. Old "work clothes" – how many sets do you need?!
16. Your tools, workshop, and garage. I spent two days going through my workshop. I sold some tools, organized scattered parts in drawer systems, and threw out a lot of old paint (colors no longer used in the house) and scrap material that I'm not sure why I saved to begin with!

What I have just described could be quite overwhelming. Remember – the key is to take one room or one project at a time. Take your time and enjoy the simplification. You will savor old memories and enjoy things a lot better when they are not in a cluttered state. Yes, you *can* do it! *I can do everything through him who gives me strength*![6]

CHAPTER FIVE

CARING FOR ELDERLY RELATIVES

> *But if a widow has children or grandchildren, these should learn first of all to put their religion into practice by caring for their own family and so repaying their parents and grandparents, for this is pleasing to God....If anyone does not provide for his relatives, and especially for his immediate family, he has denied the faith and is worse than an unbeliever.* (1 Tim. 5:4,8)

Probably most of us will have opportunities at some point to care for at least one elderly relative in a practical way. In America, this God-given responsibility has become an option, as we have so many nursing and retirement homes available – some with government Medicare assistance. In most countries in the world, it is assumed family members will take widows, the elderly, or orphans into their home when the need arises. In the opening verses, we can see that caring for relatives is a weighty matter with God.

As Jesus was experiencing all the horrific pain of hanging on a cross, he uttered an amazing statement.

> *When Jesus saw his mother there, and the disciple whom he loved standing nearby, he said to his mother, "Dear woman, here is your son," and to the disciple, "Here is your mother." From that time on, this disciple took her into his home.*[1]

Think about this – at a time of greatest suffering and agony, Jesus is thinking about the practical needs of his mother. He speaks to John, his closest disciple, about taking care of his mother after his death. This scene is a reminder to us that caring for our families is always a duty in life and ought to be a priority.

The first emphasis is that children must take the first initiative in caring for elderly parents or grandparents. *But if a widow has children or grandchildren, these should learn first of all to put their religion into practice by caring for their own family and so repaying their parents and grandparents, for this is pleasing to God.* Two words are especially relevant in this passage – the word, *learn,* and the word *repay*, or *give back.* Both of these verbs are present active, so we could translate, *they should keep on learning...keep on giving back...* [2] William Hendriksen made this observation,

> Children and grandchildren should honor their progenitors! That is their first religious duty toward those who brought them up. They should strive to make a *real return* [or *give back*] for all the care that was so lovingly bestowed upon them. Note, "Let these first learn" this lesson. By nature children are often disinclined to provide for their needy parents. According to a Dutch proverb it frequently seems easier for one poor father to bring up ten children than for ten rich children to provide for one poor father. But even if it means self-denial, this lesson must be learned. It is certainly implied in the fifth commandment (*"Honor your father and mother..."*). Moreover, it should be done with gladness, in the spirit of love, as a token of appreciation for that which the children have themselves received from their parents.[3]

The Puritan, Richard Baxter, added,

> Be sure that you dearly love your parents; delight to be in their company; be not like those unnatural children, that love the company of their idle play-fellows better than their parents, and had rather be abroad about their sports, than in their parents' sight. Remember that you have your being from them, and come out of their loins: remember what sorrow you have cost them, and what care they gave for your education and provision; and remember how tenderly they have loved you ... and how much your happiness will make them glad: remember what love you owe them both by nature and in justice, for all their love to you, and all that they have done for you: they take your happiness or misery to be one of the greatest parts of the happiness or misery of their own lives.[4]

Some of us have become more involved in caring for aging parents. As they grew older I had to care in some practical ways for my mother, an aunt, a step-grandmother, and an uncle. For about ten years, I spent considerable time looking after them. We should never feel we are wasting time or getting sidetracked when we practically help elderly relatives. It is a normal part of life. However, there are…

Some Things to Consider

1. Distance might be a factor.

Teresa's parents and relatives live four hours away from us in another state. Over the years we have tried to visit at least every couple months. Now that her mom is alone, we try to go more frequently. Teresa and I both have regular jobs and responsibilities, and our visits have to be limited. When parents are some distance away, *we will likely suffer a guilty feeling that we are not doing enough.* We must come to accept the fact that we *are* limited, and ask the Lord to bring into their lives additional friends and help. The Lord brought a very dear, caring friend into my mother's life, in her last two years at a retirement home. For Teresa's mom, a morning "breakfast club" has been a valuable support.

2. **We must not forsake our mate and children in the process of helping others.**

Wives must be especially careful in this regard. Part of their natural, God-given make-up is to be nurturing and caring – usually much more than men. Therefore, they may become so completely absorbed in caring for an elderly parent that they neglect the needs of their husband (and sometimes their children). Some ladies wear themselves out and then all the husband gets is the "left-overs" of her time and devotion. Although it will not be easy when caring for others, our mates must remain our first priority in life after our relationship with the Lord.

3. **Sometimes the best solution is *not* to have a relative live with you.**

We must always be open to making room for an elderly parent, but sometimes it just does not work out for the best. I have seen some households where it worked quite well and was a blessing to all involved. On the other hand, an extended family is not always the answer. Some elderly parents may become too demanding or be too particular about their food and lifestyle. Certain elderly mothers seem to forget their "children" are now grown adults and may revert back to the days when orders were given and little discussion allowed! All this is to suggest that we need the wisdom of God to carefully "count the cost" before inviting a relative in for a permanent arrangement.

Charles Swindoll shared about his widower dad who came to live with him and his wife, Cynthia, in his latter years.

The time came, however, when his dad needed around-the-clock nursing care.

> As we wrestled with this difficult decision, we also wrestled with guilt. But after much discussion, lots of prayer, and carefully weighing of Scripture, we realized that honoring my father didn't require us to provide his medical care *personally.* In fact, he was more comfortable with a professional taking care of the medical details while we (and my sister, Luci) remained personally involved. All the way to his death, he was treated with honor and respect. We did our best to keep him from feeling abandoned.[5]

As I mentioned in the previous chapter, Teresa and I considered having my mother stay with us. We thought of renovating our house to include a small apartment on one end to allow her privacy and yet we could plan some evening meals and times together. In the end, however, we realized my mother was used to a rather quiet, peaceful, orderly life and our lifestyle at that time was quite the opposite. We were in the midst of raising two very active pre-teen boys, who used fairly loud voices in conversations, seemed to move more at "high-speed" than "low-speed," and who constantly liked to dribble basketballs and play "rough-and-tough" with their friends in our driveway (which would have been right beside my mother's proposed living quarters). We concluded that all this activity would have been too much for her to bear, and she might have ended her days as a nervous wreck! Instead, she bought a small house on our street, and we able to give her basically the same attention we had planned. Everyone was happy!

4. **In caring for relatives, we must do *what we can* and not feel guilty about what we cannot do.**

Just as I am writing this chapter, a dear friend of ours confessed how depressed she has been feeling lately. She felt she had not spent adequate time with her mother, whose health is rapidly failing. As my wife talked to her, she sensed her friend was being condemned by Satan, *the accuser of the brothers,*[6] and encouraged her to stand in the armor of God. At times we need to remind ourselves, *Therefore, there is now no condemnation for those who are in Christ Jesus...*[7]

Whether trying to help people in our church, the community, or our own families, we must realize our limits. In balancing all our God-ordained responsibilities, we may only be able to spend so much time with an elderly relative. We may have to give our time sacrificially for a season and possibly need to enlist other help, but let's not inflict guilt upon ourselves for what we *don't* do or believe the devil's accusing lies. We must simply do what we think is right and then be at peace. Scripture says, *Blessed are those who do not condemn themselves by doing something they know is all right.*[8]

Caring For A Sick Mate

This is probably the greatest challenge to the marriage covenant that included the words "for better or *for worse.*" In latter years, sometimes a mate suffers a stroke or some other life-threatening disease, and the healthy partner suddenly finds himself/herself as a primary caretaker. Sometimes this is possible and other times nursing assistance is needed. Regardless, in such situations we will likely be called to serve at a new depth.

Every married person needs to be prepared one day to love his/her mate in a sacrificial manner, with the love of Christ – a love that can give even though nothing may be given in return. Two examples of this kind of loving care have stood out to me over the years. Both are examples of the deep love of Christ being demonstrated in very difficult circumstances.

She's My Precious[9]

By Robertson McQuilkin

(Robertson McQuilkin was the president of Columbia Bible College and Seminary. He wrote this six years after stepping down to care for his wife, Muriel, who suffered from Alzheimer's.)

Seventeen summers ago, Muriel and I began our journey into the twilight. It's midnight now, at least for her, and sometimes I wonder when dawn will break. Even the dread of Alzheimer's disease isn't supposed to attack so early and torment so long. Yet, in her silent world, Muriel is so content, so lovable. If Jesus took her home, how I would miss her gentle, sweet presence. Yes, there are times when I get irritated, but not often. It doesn't make much sense to get angry. And besides, perhaps the Lord has been answering the prayer of my youth to mellow my spirit.

Once, though, I completely lost it. In the days when Muriel could still stand and walk and we had not resorted to diapers, sometimes there were "accidents." I was on my knees beside her, trying to clean up the mess as she stood, confused, by the toilet. It would have been easier if she weren't so insistent on helping. I got more and more frustrated. Suddenly, to make her stand still, I slapped her calf – as if that would do any good. It wasn't a hard slap, but she was startled. I was, too. Never in our forty-four years of marriage had I ever so much as touched her in anger or in rebuke of any kind. Never. I wasn't even tempted, in fact. But, now, when she needed me most….

Sobbing, I pled with her to forgive me – no matter that she didn't understand words any better than she could speak them. So I turned to the Lord to tell Him how sorry I was. It took me days to get over it. Maybe God bottled those tears to quench the fires that might ignite again some day.

Recently, a student wife asked me, "Don't you ever get tired?"

"Tired? Every night. That's why I go to bed."

"No, I mean tired of..." and she tilted her head toward Muriel, who sat silently in her wheelchair, her vacant eyes saying, "No one at home just now."

I responded to Cindi's question, "Why, no, I don't get tired. I love to care for her. She's my precious...."

Love is said to evaporate if the relationship is not mutual, if it's not physical, if the other person doesn't communicate, or if one party doesn't carry his or her share of the load. When I hear the litany of essentials for a happy marriage, I count off what my beloved can no longer contribute, and then I contemplate how truly mysterious love is.

What some people find so hard to understand is that loving Muriel isn't hard. They wonder about my former loves – like my work.

"Do you miss being president?" a student asked as we sat in our little garden. I told him I'd never thought about it, but on reflection, no. As exhilarating as my work has been, I enjoyed learning to cook and keep house. No, I'd never looked back.

I think my life is happier than the lives of 95 percent of the people on planet earth.

Love for the Unresponding[10]

By Dr. Ed Wheat

(Dr. Ed Wheat is a popular marriage counselor and has authored best selling books like Intended For Pleasure *and* Love Life.)

A man loved his wife tenderly and steadfastly for a total of fifteen years without any responding love on her part. There could be no response, for she had developed cerebral arteriosclerosis, the chronic brain syndrome....At the onset of the disease she was a pretty, vivacious lady of sixty who looked at least ten years younger. In the beginning she experienced intermittent times of confusion....As the disease progressed, she gradually lost all her mental faculties and did not even recognize her husband. He took care of her at home by himself for the first five years. During that time he often took her for visits, she looking her prettiest although she had no idea of where she was, and he proudly displaying her as his wife, introducing her to everyone, even though her remarks were apt to be inappropriate to the conversation. He never made an apology for her; he never indicated that there was anything wrong with what she had just said. He always treated her with the utmost courtesy. He showered her with love and attention, no matter what she said or did….The time came when the doctors said she had to go into a nursing home for intensive care. She lived there for ten years (part of that time bedfast with arthritis) and he was with her daily....He never made a negative comment about her. He did not begrudge the large amount of money required to keep her in the home all those years, never even hinted that it might be a problem. In fact, he never complained about any detail of her care throughout the long illness....This man was loyal, always true to his wife, even though his love had no response for fifteen years….I can speak of this case with intimate knowledge, for these people were my own wonderful parents. What my father taught me about *agape* love through his example I can never forget."

Both of these amazing examples – Ed Wheat's father and Robertson McQuilkin – certainly model the very love of God. Christian love often shines the brightest when there is no response or gratitude from the recipient. As we read these examples, the question arises – "How could I ever do that?" Well, not one of us could do it without *the grace of God* in our hearts and *the power of the Holy Spirit* to demonstrate God's own love through us. As it has been said, God gives us suffering grace in times of suffering, and when such love is needed from us, God can manifest supernatural love through us – far beyond our limited, human capacity.

Great Patience is Also Required

I have found that in assisting elderly relatives, my love and patience have been sorely tested. But, I have seen this fruit of the Spirit develop in my life, and – thanks be to God – I am much more patient than I used to be. One motivator for me to be patient with others is to realize God's incredible patience with me. If my loving Savior has been so patient with my failings and shortcomings, time after time, should not I also be patient with others? There are a multitude of ways we will need to demonstrate this quality with elderly people. For example…

- Do I listen well – even though I may have heard them tell the same story several times before?
- Do I forbear (put up with) irritating habits? Scripture says, ...*with patience, bearing with one another* and *making allowances because you love one another.*[11]
- Do I overlook childish or even stubborn behavior? (*Love covers a multitude of sins…*[12])
- Do I graciously clean up their messes?
- Do I slowly and patiently try to reason with them, even when they resist the change that is coming?

Wise Advice From Billy Graham

In January 2011, Billy Graham – at the ripe age of ninety-two – was interviewed by *Christianity Today* on the subject of aging. One of the questions he was asked was, "What would you say to children who have aging parents?" His answer is very wise.

> The first thing I'd say to those whose parents are growing older is to be prepared for it, and to accept whatever responsibilities it brings you. Then be patient with them. They may not be able to do

everything they once did, but that doesn't mean they're necessarily helpless or incompetent. And be alert to their needs – including their emotional and spiritual needs. Sometimes they just need to know that you're there, and that you care. Be sensitive also. Occasionally I've seen children become heavy-handed and insensitive when dealing with their aging parents, and it only caused resentment and hard feelings. On the other hand, it may become necessary to step in and insist that they turn over the car keys, or let you handle their finances, or even arrange for them to move to a place where they'll get better care. They may resist, and you need to put yourself in their shoes and realize the turmoil these changes can cause them. But they need to realize that you're doing it because you love them and want what's best for them. And pray for them also, that they will experience God's peace and comfort as they grow older. Some day you'll be there also, and what you do now will be an example to your own children.[13]

Wise advice indeed. We must always remember the "Golden Rule" when caring for aging parents – treat them in the same manner we would hope to be personally treated as we grow older. That ought to cause us to be very careful and patient.

We will close this chapter with a popular poem that we can take as a personal plea from our elderly relatives for greater understanding, love, and patience from us in the days ahead.

A Grandmother's Beatitudes[14]

By Esther Mary Walker

Blessed are those who understand
My faltering step and palsied hand.

Blessed are those who know that my ears today
Must strain to catch the things they say.

Blessed are those who seem to know
That my eyes are dim and my wits are slow.

Blessed are those who looked away
When coffee spilled at table today.

Blessed are those with a cheery smile
Who stop to chat for a little while.

Blessed are those who never say,
"You've told that story twice today."

Blessed are those who know the ways
To bring back memories of yesterdays.

Blessed are those who make it known
That I'm loved, respected, and not alone.

Blessed are those who know I'm at a loss
To find the strength to carry the Cross.

Blessed are those who ease the days
On my journey Home in loving ways.

CHAPTER SIX

WATCHING OVER WIDOWS

Religion that God our Father accepts as pure and faultless is this: to look after orphans and widows in their distress and to keep oneself from being polluted by the world. (James 1:27)

This is one of the most surprising verses in the Bible. If people on the street (or even in many churches) were randomly surveyed about the most important aspects of their religion, how many would answer, "caring for widows and orphans"? As I searched many popular Bible topical books in this study, very few list the word "widow" in their subjects. Yet, this theme of *looking after orphans and widows* seems to be extremely important in the priorities of God and is a chief characteristic of *pure religion.*

Our First Responsibility – Compassion and Comfort for the Grieving

When someone loses a loved one, our first responsibility is to lovingly embrace them and minister the compassion of Jesus. No one on earth can fathom the pain and sorrow when a husband or wife loses their faithful friend, lover, and constant companion – in some cases, a person with whom they have shared intimate life together for more than half a century. The Bible says, *Each heart knows its own bitterness, and no one else can fully share its joy.*[1] Each person on earth is a unique creation of God; as individuals we will grieve in different ways. Some folks will show little emotion at the loss of a mate, although it is apparent they deeply miss the departed one. Others seem to sorrow on a deeper level and walk in grief for years. We must avoid any judgments in such cases and allow each person to grieve in his/her own way.

Vance Havner, former chaplain to the U.S. Senate, wrote a precious book about the death of Sara, his dear wife of thirty-three years. In *Though I Walk Through the Valley,* Havner candidly writes about his grief following her death.

> One thing is certain when your dearest leaves you for heaven and you plod on alone – there can be no harder blow, no greater human bereavement. After this any other adversities, any other tragedies, any other disasters will be secondary. You have had the worst. Whatever happens to you personally is incidental. Much of the darkness of death disappears for it becomes the door to a glad reunion….
>
> There has been profound human grief of which I am not ashamed. I would be ashamed if I didn't have it. There have been tears aplenty but I am assured that one day God Himself will wipe them all away. They are preserved in His bottle and recorded in His Book (see Psalms 56:8). But there has been joy unspeakable and full of glory as we trust Him "though now we see Him not, yet believing" (see 1 Peter 1:8).
>
> Tonight I sit in this lonely apartment. I would give just about everything if we could sit once more and enjoy a favorite television program. Things once taken for granted loom large now. I would say to every husband and wife, "Count no day unimportant if you still have each other, for the day will come when you would give everything for just one day, any ordinary day, you once shared together."[2]

Because grief for a husband or wife is so profound, we must respond to hurting people in caring compassion. Especially in the early stages of grief, our words ought to be few. I have learned in many cases that just giving a hug is the best way I can minister to a grieving one.

In deciding how to minister effectively to those who are grieving, Lauren Briggs has offered helpful guidelines. She said we should not minimize a friend's pain with comments like, "It's probably for the best." "Things could be worse." "You'll remarry." "You're strong, you'll get over it soon." "You know God is in control." Comments like these might be an attempt to offer hope, but to a hurting person, they sound as though you don't comprehend the enormity of what's happened – they don't acknowledge their pain and loss.

Instead, it is much better to offer simple, understanding statements such as: "I feel for you during this difficult time." "This must be very hard for you." "I share your feelings of loss." Comments like these let the person know you acknowledge their pain and it's okay for them to feel that way.[3]

People who are grieving don't need "fixing," nor do they need an onslaught of biblical advice. They simply need our compassion and understanding, and in months to come, they will especially need our friendship. We must not ignore their needs after the immediate loss has subsided.

The Church – a Caring Family

When the Bible says we must *look after orphans and widows in their distress,* the expression, *look after,* is translated *visit* by the New American Standard Bible, but the Greek word means more here than a mere social call; it means to care for, provide for, to examine carefully the need.[4] It is found in Jesus' statement, *"I was sick and you looked after me."*[5]

Sometimes, when a husband or wife loses his/her mate, they have no living close relatives or no relatives who live close enough to be any practical help. In such cases the church must rise to the occasion and help. (In this chapter I will use "widow" but we also realize that "widowers" suffer in the same way and need attention as well.)

God never intended his church to become a cold institution run like a smooth operating business, nor should it be a "social club" – a clique of favorite friends who enjoy like-minded company. The church ought to be more like a family: *Now you are no longer strangers to God and foreigners to heaven, but you are members of God's very own family, citizens of God's country, and you belong in God's household with every other Christian.*[6]

In an authentic church, we should find a caring group of believers, who deliberately reach out to the needy in a sincere and compassionate way. The Bible especially commends those who reach out to orphans and widows.

In ancient Israel, God's people were commanded to look after widows and orphans and not to take advantage of them.

> *Do not take advantage of a widow or an orphan. If you do and they cry out to me, I will certainly hear their cry. My anger will be aroused, and I will kill you with the sword; your wives will become widows and your children fatherless.*[7]

> *Cursed is the man who withholds justice from the alien, the fatherless or the widow.*[8]

> *Learn to do right! Seek justice, encourage the oppressed. Defend the cause of the fatherless, plead the case of the widow.*[9]

In Jesus' day many religious folks avoided the widows, but Jesus showed much tender compassion and practical care. He noticed the widow who contributed two small coins to the temple treasury.[10] His "heart went out" to a widow who had lost her only son, and he commanded the dead boy to come back to life.[11] As we mentioned in the last chapter, Jesus thought about the care of his widowed mother, Mary, even while hanging on the cross.[12]

With the baby-boomer generation coming into "retirement age," the church ought to have plentiful opportunities to assist solitary widows. The Bible is very practical here, and offers some…

Instructions for Helping Widows

A local church must be a good steward – both of its time and money invested in needy people. The early Christians were not a communistic group that just unilaterally divided up property and helped everybody who seemed to have a need. No, they were led by the Holy Spirit and excluded some people from practical assistance. Notice Paul's instructions about helping widows:

> *Give proper recognition to those widows who are really in need. But if a widow has children or grandchildren, these should learn first of all to put their religion into practice by caring for their own family and so repaying their parents and grandparents, for this is pleasing to God. The widow who is really in need and left all alone puts her hope in God and continues night and day to pray and to ask God for help. But the widow who lives for pleasure is dead even while she lives….If anyone does not provide for his relatives, and especially for his immediate family, he has denied the faith and is worse than an unbeliever.*
>
> *No widow may be put on the list of widows unless she is over sixty, has been faithful to her husband, and is well known for her good deeds, such as bringing up children, showing hospitality, washing the feet of the saints, helping those in trouble and*

devoting herself to all kinds of good deeds. As for younger widows, do not put them on such a list. For when their sensual desires overcome their dedication to Christ, they want to marry...So I counsel younger widows to marry, to have children, to manage their homes and to give the enemy no opportunity for slander...

If any woman who is a believer has widows in her family, she should help them and not let the church be burdened with them, so that the church can help those widows who are really in need.[13]

In the previous chapter we discussed the priority of children helping their needy parents or grandparents. When there is no family to help, then certain limitations come into play. If the local church is helping widows today, we might not need to follow these exact biblical details. (For example, does she need to wash the feet of other believers?) But certain guidelines we may want to include:

- Is she still young? Can she remarry?
- Doe she have family or relatives to help her?
- Does she need financial help from the church? (If her husband left her a substantial insurance policy, she may not need such help.)
- Is she active in the church, serving God's people, or is she just an occasional visitor?

John MacArthur has encouraged the church to become engaged in helping widows.

> We live in a country that provides some basic coverage for widows. But the scope of their needs is increasing. Some widows might desire a Christian education for their children, and the church could set

> up a scholarship fund toward meeting that need. Other widows may have previously lived on a low income while others may have lived on a higher one. So the church will need to exercise wisdom to determine which needs are real ones.
>
> The church must be committed to widows who genuinely need assistance, whatever the cost might be. It may mean transferring money out of optional church programs so basic needs can be met. The church should be happy to do that because it shows God's compassion toward the destitute. Even when widows have financial resources, the church needs to come alongside with encouragement, love, and support in every way possible.
>
> The increasing collapse of the family unit in our society means there will be an increase in the number of widows that need to be under the church's care. For instance, a Christian widow with several children might not receive any help from unsaved parents. It would be good if she could move back into her parents' home (Gen. 38:11), but that is not always possible... The church needs to discern which widows are in genuine need of financial care. It cannot indiscriminately give to everyone.[14]

Spiritual discernment is an important key in any help we offer. Rather than setting a rigid policy of whom we help as a church family, we should take each widow as a unique case, and seek the wisdom of God. This is one good reason to consider...

The Role of Deacons

Deacons have different functions in different churches. Many biblical scholars see the first example of functioning New Testament deacons in the book of Acts, chapter six. This was a time of unusual church growth and certain widows were being overlooked in the distribution of food. So the twelve apostles selected some godly and wise men in their midst, to take responsibility for this task.

Deacons ought to be more than just caretakers of buildings and grounds; they ought to be involved in the care of people as well. In his excellent book, *The New Testament Deacon,* Alexander Strauch called deacons the church's "ministers of mercy."

> Through the deacons, the local church's charitable activities are effectively organized and centralized. The deacons are collectors of funds, distributors of relief, and agents of mercy. They help the poor, the jobless, the sick, the widowed, the elderly, the homeless, the shut-in, the refugees, and the disabled. They counsel and guide people. They visit people in their homes. They relieve suffering. They comfort, protect, and encourage people, and help to meet their needs. In contemporary language, they are the congregation's social workers.[15]

In our own church we feel our ministry of deacons is still in transition. Over the years we have selected eight men as deacons. Some of these men specialize in finances, some in building maintenance, and some in other practical services. However, *all* are instructed to make *people* the first priority. Once a month a couple of our pastors meet with all the deacons, and we usually review a list of widows and other needy people. We verify that certain individuals are staying in touch with them and that their needs are not being overlooked. Some of this oversight may include organizing work parties to assist in yard or house work. We ask each deacon to pray and consider any specific people he might check on. We have also established a "benevolence fund" with a budgeted amount of money set aside each month to assist widows or other needy people in our congregation.

We are still "feeling our way" but are encouraging our deacons to prepare now, so that when greater needs arise in the future, we will be more prepared to act.

Are We Being Hospitable?

> *Above all, love each other deeply, because love covers over a multitude of sins. Offer hospitality to one another without grumbling.*[16]

The Greek word for *hospitality* is a compound word that combines a common word for "love" with the word used for "strangers." In other words, hospitality – at the root – means a "love for strangers." Some believers think that "church" is meeting with a few couples they like in their living room. This is an extremely limited view of church, because in God's household we will find people from different social and economic backgrounds, and we must be willing to mix with people "outside our box." If the only people we ever share a meal with or talk with are our close friends, we know little of true biblical fellowship.

As financial times get harder in our country, I believe we will have greater opportunities to help each other in many practical ways. This demonstration of love will indicate if we are truly a church family. Will we even consider opening our homes to take in a widow (or a needy single brother or sister in Christ)? Not all families will be able to do such a thing, but I know some families who are making preparations in their homes now for such future possibilities.

Even small acts of love can make a difference. Consider taking a widow out to lunch or supper, or including her (or him) in a family activity. Often following a death of a spouse, the remaining one has an onslaught of calls, food, and cards. Then, after a month, there is little attention, and life can feel pretty lonely. God has a solution for the lonely one: *God sets the lonely in families.*[17] May we all be open to the Holy Spirit's guidance in reaching out to the widows he has connected us with.

CHAPTER SEVEN

EMBRACING GOD'S BEST PROMISES FOR OLD AGE

In his goodness, God has given us his very *great and precious promises.*[1] The promises, if embraced as God's personal word to us, are meant to sustain and encourage us – even to the end of our lives. Billy Graham once stated,

> Old age has its compensations. More than ever I see each day as a gift from God. It is also a time to reflect back on God's goodness over the years and an opportunity to assure others that God is truly faithful to his promises.[2]

There are a multitude of promises from God's word that apply to believers of all ages, but there are seven that seem to be especially applicable for those entering their latter years.

Promise #1
God Will Sustain Us

> *Even to your old age and gray hairs I am he, I am he who will sustain you. I have made you and I will carry you; I will sustain you and I will rescue you. (Is.46:4)*

This is an especially good promise for elderly folks who feel neglected. The One who created us will not abandon us; he has promised to *sustain* us and to *carry* us. What a wonderful promise! Elsewhere the Bible says, *...the LORD your God carried you, as a father carries his son, all the way you went until you reached this place.*[3] *Cast your burden upon the LORD and He will sustain you; He will never allow the righteous to be shaken.*[4] Even when family members forsake us and friends forget all about us, *the Lord will take care of us.*[5] The Lord Himself has promised to be *our refuge and strength, an ever-present help in trouble.*[6]

Promise #2
God Will Keep Us Here Until His Perfect Time

> *You will live to a good old age. You will not be harvested until the proper time! (Job 5:26 NLT)*

This is a great promise for any of us who have felt close to death: God will not take us home until his proper time! Another verse states the same truth. *My times are in your hands; deliver me from my enemies and from those who pursue me.*[7] Henry Martyn was an outstanding pioneer missionary to India in the early nineteenth century. He often faced physical sickness and dangers, often to the point of death. He once declared, "If God has work for me to do, I cannot die."[8] This great confession ought to be on the lips of every one of us. We can say, "As long as God wants me here and I can in some way be useful to his kingdom and a blessing to other people, I will not die, but live!" This was the bold declaration of the psalmist, *I will not die but live, and will proclaim what the LORD has done.*[9]

Promise #3
God is at Work in All Our Circumstances

> *And we know that in all things God works for the good of those who love him, who have been called according to his purpose. (Rom. 8:28)*

I believe this is the most encouraging verse in the Bible for believers at any age. No matter what family problems, health issues, or financial strains we encounter, God is still at work for our good. He has not abandoned us!

R.A. Torrey was a renowned Bible teacher in the ninteenth century, and the first president of Moody Bible Institute. When he was about seventy years old, he could barely speak and it became difficult for him even to swallow. He had to forego his normal diet and his weight dropped from 225 to 150 pounds. During this time his wife, always tender and sympathetic, said, "Poor Archie. You must be discouraged. Your poor throat." Her husband replied militantly with paper and pencil, "Discouraged – nothing! Romans 8:28 is more precious to me than ever before."[10] To him, his failing health was one of "all things." He didn't especially relish any inquiries about his health. His reply was always positive – "improving." Torrey's son, Reuben, later mentioned that during this time of declining health, his father "demonstrated the completeness of his victory in Christ Jesus...he never manifested the slightest impatience...His beautiful smile persisted...his faith and glad acceptance of God's will became more evident. He gave himself to almost continuous Bible study and prayer, and his very presence was a benediction."[11]

Promise #4
God Will Deliver Us From Fear

> *Even though I walk through the valley of the shadow of death, I will fear no evil, for you are with me; your rod and your staff, they comfort me. (Ps.23:4)*

What is *the valley of the shadow of death*? A shadow implies the real thing is not far away, so I believe David was saying these are times in which danger and death are close at hand. I like the word "shadow" – the shadow of a dog cannot bite; the shadow of a sword cannot kill, and the shadow of death cannot harm the child of God until God's allotted time.[12]

An alternative translation in most Bible margins is *through the darkest valley.* We might prefer to walk *around* the darkest valley, but we often have to walk *through* it. What has been your darkest valley to this point in life? A health issue? A lost job? Your reputation smeared? How about the loss of a family member? I have heard many Christians testify at funerals, and I am amazed how the Good Shepherd has been very real to them in such a time of need.

The reason we never need to fear the dark valley is very simple - the Good Shepherd always walks beside us - even when we do not feel his presence. He has said, *"I will never leave you or forsake you."*[13] *"And surely I am with you always, to the very end of the age."*[14] Philip Keller has written about this in his excellent book, *A Shepherd Looks at Psalm 23.* He said when he was working with sheep, "I came to realize that nothing so quieted and reassured the sheep as to see me in the field."[15] This is good news indeed – our Good Shepherd is in our field, and He has promised to walk with us through the darkest valley.

Promise #5
God Will Still Use Us in Our Older Years

> *The righteous man... will still yield fruit in old age; they shall be full of sap and very green, to declare that the LORD is upright; He is my rock, and there is no unrighteousness in Him. (Ps. 92:12-15 NAS)*

What great words for the righteous in their old age! In this portion of Scripture we see four splendid promises:

- We will be *full of sap.* This speaks of spiritual vitality. The Hebrew word used here means, "fat, juicy, prosperous, rich; being healthy spiritually from God's blessings."[16]

- We will still be *very green.* This expression implies we can still flourish; we are not quite ready to wither! This Hebrew word means, "green, flourishing; it refers to a luxuriant plant or tree, flourishing and full of vibrant life."[17]

- We will *still yield fruit.* God is not finished with us yet – there is still more work to be done! This is especially encouraging for those who have not served Christ in their prime years; we can still bear fruit in the end! In a later chapter, we will look at numerous examples of people who were quite fruitful in their latter years.

- We can maintain our testimony. Even if health declines or we face other trials related to aging, we can still boldly declare, *"The LORD is upright; He is my rock, and there is no unrighteousness in Him!"*

Promise #6
God Will Finish the Work He Began in Us

> *Being confident of this, that he who began a good work in you will carry it on to completion until the day of Christ Jesus. (Phil.1:6)*

We believe we are saved by grace – from beginning to end! We are thankful Jesus is our Lord and Savior – *the beginning and the end.*[18] He has promised to do his work in us – to the very end! It is God who *works in you to will and to act according to his good purpose.*[19] We are not some piece of shoddy, unfinished artwork that will be set aside. We are *continually his workmanship, his work of art.*[20] The Master Craftsman has a beautiful masterpiece in mind that he fully intends to bring to completion. Praise His name!

Promise #7
God's Goodness and Mercy Will Pursue Us to the End

> *Surely goodness and mercy shall follow me all the days of my life; And I will dwell in the house of the Lord forever. (Ps. 23:6 NKJV)*

God has given us two constant companions – his goodness and mercy. An alternative translation reads that these two attributes of God *will pursue me all the days of my life…*[21] Someone has called *goodness and mercy* God's two "sheepdogs" – always following us, and when we are going the wrong direction, they are nipping at our heels.

The goodness of God is his kindness, expressed in such a gracious, benevolent, and abundant manner, that we can hardly avoid it. It is the goodness of God that draws us to the Lord and *leads us to repentance.*[22] It is the goodness of God that sustains us. King David said, *I would have despaired unless I had believed that I would see the goodness of the LORD in the land of the living.*[23]

The mercy of God is his love and compassion shown to a pitiful and powerless person, a person who is expecting just the opposite, and one who certainly does not deserve such wonderful forgiveness and forbearance.

Aren't we glad that these two "sheepdogs" will keep "nipping at our heels" – not just for a while – but for *all the days of our lives?* The goodness and mercy of God are not just seasonal blessings, nor do they stop when we reach seventy or eighty. *Oh, give thanks to the Lord, for He is good! For His mercy endures forever.*[24]

Yes, we can have confidence the Lord our God will look after us and keep us – even to the end of our days. With such assurance we can say, *I will dwell in the house of the Lord forever!*

CHAPTER EIGHT

MAINTAINING A JOYFUL AND GRATEFUL HEART

It can be confirmed – both biblically and medically – that those who maintain an optimistic, joyful, and grateful heart not only tend to live longer, but also enjoy their latter years much more than those with a pessimistic and ungrateful disposition.

These three simple Scriptures ought to especially characterize believers who are growing older.

> *A cheerful heart is good medicine, but a crushed spirit dries up the bones. (Prov.17:22)*
>
> *A joyful heart makes a cheerful face, but when the heart is sad, the spirit is broken. (Prov. 15:13 NAS)*
>
> *Always be joyful. Keep on praying. No matter what happens, always be thankful, for this is God's will for you who belong to Christ Jesus. (1 Th. 5:16-18 NLT)*

Medical Benefits

Dr. Don Colbert, when asked how a "cheerful heart" can be "good medicine," commented that people with a good sense of humor have "less stress and better health." He then recommended at least ten hearty laughs a day! Colbert also shared some results from medical research.

Dr. Lee Berk of Loma Linda University Medical Center in California concluded that laughter boosts the immune system and reduces dangerous stress hormones.

Cortisol, a stress hormone, fell thirty-nine percent and adrenaline seventy percent among sixteen men in one study who had a good belly laugh while watching a funny video. Cortisol is a dangerous hormone that, once elevated for an extended time, becomes like acid in the body. It especially affects the brain, eventually causing memory loss.

Berk reported that laughter helps the immune system by increasing:

- Immunoglobulin A, which helps protect against respiratory infections.
- Gamma interferon, the immune system's front-line defense against viruses.
- B cells that produce antibodies to fight harmful bacteria.
- Complement 2, a combination of proteins that is a catalyst in antibody reactions.

Colbert also said that a "merry heart" can lower blood pressure as well, and that a research team at the University of Maryland reported in 2000 that people who exercise humor are less likely to suffer a heart attack.[1]

Few People Enjoy the Company of a Complainer

When you think of the people you enjoy spending time with, are not most of them vibrant, optimistic, and happy people? Most of us are not naturally drawn to negative, woeful complainers.

I can remember one elderly relative that whenever I asked her how she was, she responded, "Worse!" After a while, I changed my tactics. When I entered her room, I smiled and asked very enthusiastically, "It's a great day today, isn't it!? Her demeanor seemed to change a little and she generally gave a weak reply, "I reckon." She seemed to respond more favorably to my joyful outlook.

Those who constantly complain will likely find few friends. Stanley Baldwin said, "When we complain, ninety percent of the people don't care and don't want to hear it; the other ten percent probably feel a secret satisfaction that we are getting what we deserve."[2]

The older we get, the more we will be tempted to complain about our aches, pains, and misfortunes. However, we must determine, instead, to *do all things without grumbling*[3] and to habitually give thanks to God for all his blessings. John Calvin stated, "The more God has lengthened our days, the more we should be exercised in singing his praises."[4] Hannah Whitall Smith added, "The soul who gives thanks can find comfort in everything; the soul who complains can find comfort in nothing."[5] At every stage of life, we cannot escape the command of Scripture: *Be joyful always …give thanks in all circumstances…*[6]

Now, let us take encouragement from several senior saints, who have modeled for us a joyful and grateful spirit.

Judson Cornwall

Judson Cornwall was a popular pastor and prolific author of more than fifty books, including best-selling books on praise and worship, like *Let Us Praise.* In 2002 Cornwall was diagnosed with an inoperable, malignant tumor on his spine. Despite the doctors telling him he only had months to live, he actually lived three more years, dying February 11, 2005 at the age of eighty. During his remaining years, Cornwall penned his last book, *Dying With Grace.* Indeed, despite the great difficulties, he walked out what he wrote in this book.

When asked what she observed about his dying process, Cornwall's long-time assistant, Terri Gargis, responded, "It's been different with Judson, because all the time he's been dying, he's been keeping the joy of the Lord. He is dying with grace, and he does it with joy."[7]

Cornwall's wife of sixty-one years, Eleanor, said, "he never complained about anything while he was sick."[8]

In his book, Cornwall is realistic about the unpleasantness of old age and facing imminent death. He also talked about his struggles with inner anger and bitter thoughts, and the eventual conclusion at which he arrived. Here are his thoughts.

> If you will focus on God's blessings in your life instead of your sickness, then there will be rejoicing in that you are still alive instead of being angry and bitter. It's sad to spend our lives majoring on the negatives. God has done so much for us that we should be grateful and filled with thanksgiving for what He has done, rather than be resentful and bitter about what He has not done.
>
> The antidote to anger and bitterness is thanksgiving. Perhaps one of the most positive by-products of giving thanks to God is that it refocuses our perspectives by causing us to look to Jesus. As we give thanks, we look away from self, from success, from failure, from ambition, and from circumstances. Thanksgiving moves us from negative thinking into positive thinking. Expressing thanks to God for what He has already done for you will release negatives from your heart and mind and replace them with positives.[9]

We can learn a lot from Cornwall's attitude!

Paul Knopp

Paul Knopp was the founding pastor of my home church in Staunton, Virginia – Community Fellowship Church. In the early 1970's Paul and Christine Knopp ("Papa" and "Mama") and their nine sons began hosting a church in their home for at least ten years. I was privileged to serve with Paul and three other men as fellow elders for over twenty-five years.

For all who knew this man, he was characterized by one outstanding trait – the joy of the Lord. I don't know if I ever had a conversation with Paul when he did not smile or quote a Scripture. He loved the word of God, and it was like a fountain of joy for him. Some of his favorite life verses included:

- *Rejoice always...in everything give thanks...* [10]
- *... the joy of the LORD is your strength.*[11]
- *For the kingdom of God is ...joy in the Holy Spirit.*[12]

I dedicated this book to Papa and Mama Knopp, because both of these dear saints modeled for hundreds of people over the years not only how to walk with Christ, but also how to grow old in the grace of God. I do not intentionally exclude Mama in my comments, but I speak more of Papa simply because I spent so much time with him. Also, he went to be with the Lord (Nov. 17, 2008) just short of his 95th birthday. He radiated the joy of the Lord to the end. The large number of people at his memorial service was a true testimony to the work of Jesus Christ in an earthen vessel.

I asked his wife and one of the sons recently if they ever saw Papa acting grumpy and complaining. They said he experienced irritations common to all mankind and would sometimes voice his frustration, but they could only recall one specific time in which he "lost his joy." Once, when his children were quite young, he was driving the entire family on a long trip – nine boys and his wife in one car! The boys were apparently being quite active and noisy, and things must have escalated to the "boiling point," because he suddenly scolded them all harshly. The family then became very quiet and the car continued on. After going a short distance, Paul pulled the car off the road and turned to the back seat. He said, "Boys, I must apologize. I haven't acted like a Christian today. I must ask your forgiveness." This incident was the only one they could remember in the sixty years of family life in which he "lost his cool!"

I asked Christine what the "secret" was to the joy Paul had discovered. She said it was something that one simply cannot create by one's own effort. After striving in his own strength for many years as a younger pastor, Paul came to the place of deeper *abiding* in Christ,[13] and a trust that only "*the Lord* could build the house."[14] He had discovered that Jesus' yoke is *easy* and his burden *light*.[15] Therefore, he could enter into the rest of the Lord and be delivered from a performance mentality. He also began to personally experience the *power* of the Holy Spirit. *"Not by might nor by power, but by my Spirit," says the LORD Almighty.*[16]

CHRISTINE AND PAUL KNOPP (MAMA AND PAPA)

Paul Knopp helped many younger believers, including myself, develop a great perspective of the Christian life. I don't think I have ever met a more joyful man.

R.C. Chapman

Although not well known today, Robert Chapman was a widely respected Christian leader in nineteenth century England, and a man whom Charles Spurgeon once described as "the saintliest man I ever knew." At the age of ninety-eight, one of Chapman's guests described him as disciplined, enthusiastic, and mentally vigorous:

> On the Lord's Day, instead of appearing exhausted after his [Saturday] fast, at his advanced age, he seems fresher than ever. I heard him exclaim, with exuberant joyfulness, to one of his friends, "The Lord is risen indeed, my brother; the Lord is risen indeed!" He comes to breakfast on such occasions with his soul filled and bubbling over with heavenly matters of praise and thanksgiving, which he pours into the ears and hearts of his listeners at the table. He is most entertaining, keeping up a genial and edifying conversation with his friends, and laughing very heartily when any amusing anecdote is related to him.... The beams from his cheerful countenance fall upon all alike, he having no favorites.[17]

May God grant us the same spirit as we grow older and may we be "fresher than ever!"

Tim Hansel

Tim Hansel, a mountain climber, once fell the height of three stories and landed on his neck. Miraculously he survived, but for over twenty years he lived with chronic pain. In his book, *You Gotta Keep Dancin'; In the Midst of Life's Hurts You Can Choose Joy,* Hansel wrote,

> Whereas happiness is a feeling, joy is an attitude...Pain is inevitable, but misery is optional. We cannot avoid pain, but we can avoid joy. God has given us such immense freedom that he will allow us to be as miserable as we want to be.
>
> I know some people who spend their entire lives practicing being unhappy, diligently pursuing joylessness. They get more mileage from having people feel sorry for them than from choosing to live out their lives in the context of joy.
>
> Joy is simple (not to be confused with easy). At any moment in life we have at least two options, and one of them is to choose an attitude of gratitude, a posture of grace, a commitment to joy.[18]

If a man with a broken body like Tim Hansel can choose joy, then what is stopping us from doing the same?

Being Content in the Latter Season of Life

While we may not be able to change the many inevitable facets of growing old, we can learn contentment. The apostle Paul, writing as an older man from a wretched prison cell, said, *I have learned to be content whatever the circumstances.*[19] Being content means we can be satisfied (and even happy) in the place and time in which we find ourselves, placing all our concerns and cares in the hands of our loving God.

Billy Graham offered this advice to those who are growing older:

> First, accept it as part of God's plan for your life, and thank him every day for the gift of that day. We've come to look on old age as something to be dreaded – and it's true that it isn't easy. I can't honestly say that

> I like being old – not being able to do most of the things I used to do, for example, and being more dependent on others, and facing physical challenges that I know will only get worse. Old age can be a lonely time also – children scattered, spouse and friends gone. But God has a reason for keeping us here (even if we don't always understand it), and we need to recover the Bible's understanding of life and longevity as gifts from God – and therefore as something good. Several times the Bible mentions people who died "at a *good* old age" – an interesting phrase (emphasis added). So part of my advice is to learn to be content, and that only comes as we accept each day as a gift from God and commit it into his hands. Paul's words are true at every stage of life, but especially as we grow older: "Godliness with contentment is great gain" (1 Tim. 6:6).[20]

What Do You Want For your Birthday?

Elisabeth Elliot shared a letter she once received from an eighty-nine year old lady, who was asked by a grandson, "What do you want for your birthday, Gramma?" Here is her written response.

> What do I need? On my 89th birthday? How about a grateful heart? A heart that is thankful for the fresh air after the much-needed rain. A heart that counts blessings too numerous to list, which I've already mentioned to God. I'm forgetting names, and when I recall them, I forget how to spell them. But I'm alive!
>
> I have another day before me when I can keep cool in the face of distraction and irritation. Let it be a day when I can touch routine with the sheer happiness of serving You, Lord. Let it be a day of praise for the loving kindness You show, for the strength and power You lend to my life, for the

unexpected joys that bless the hours, and for Your Spirit's presence.

That's what I want for my birthday, and every day. A grateful heart.[21]

May we, too, have that same wonderful attitude! "That's what I want for my birthday, and every day. A grateful heart." We must even expand that request to a "joyful and grateful heart." May God grant us our heart's desire!

CHAPTER NINE

FACING DEATH WITH AN OPTIMISTIC FAITH

There is a time for everything,
and a season for every activity under heaven:
a time to be born and a time to die...
(Ecclesiastes 3:1-2)

Death is a relevant subject for every one of us. The statistics on death are very simple: one out of one people die. C. S. Lewis wryly stated, "War does not increase death... Death is total in every generation. Everybody dies."[1]

People generally avoid the subject of death. Somehow we think we will be an exception to an untimely death, or that death for me is a long way off. But the Bible is clear, *It is appointed for men to die once, but after this the judgment...*[2] *Moreover, no man knows when his hour will come...*[3] We prefer not to think about unpleasant realities – especially death and the judgment to come. However, having a biblical view of death is essential – especially the older we get. As believers in Christ, we need not be depressed about our future; we can face death with an optimistic faith! So, let us be encouraged as we consider...

The Christian View of Death

1. Death is a continuation of Christ's lordship.

When we declare, "Jesus is Lord," do we ever connect our confession with death? I have shared the following verses at many funerals I have conducted.

> *For none of us lives to himself alone and none of us dies to himself alone. If we live, we live to the Lord; and if we die, we die to the Lord. So, whether we live or die, we belong to the Lord. For this very reason, Christ died and returned to life so that he might be the Lord of both the dead and the living.*[4]

This is a most encouraging statement – *So, whether we live or die, we belong to the Lord.* J. B. Phillips has an interesting translation of these verses:

> *At every turn life links us to the Lord and when we die we come face to face with him. In life and death we are in the hands of the Lord; Christ lived and died that he might be Lord in both life and death.*[5]

Stop and think for a moment, "What is Christianity? It is living – really living – under the lordship of Christ. It is not just spiritually getting by with the least commitment and involvement and then sneaking our way into heaven. No, it is living under Jesus' lordship...and after death, his reign and relationship with us continues. Jesus said, *He who believes in me will live, even though he dies.*"[6]

2. **Death is gain. (Phil. 1:21)**

Let's suppose a believer – who is very close to us – suddenly dies. We will sorrow, but remember – it is only *our* loss, not his/her loss. Now, for all of eternity, that person will no longer suffer all the pains, frustrations, miseries, sorrows, and disappointments that accompany one's life in this world. That person will now be in the company of Jesus and have a fellowship and joy which far exceeds anything he could possibly have here on earth. So, if a dear Christian friend dies, we should not sorrow too long! When a believer dies, it is gain! The Phillips translation says, *"If I die I should merely gain more of him."*[7]

When Derek Prince lost his wife, Ruth, he sent out an announcement that read, "Now That Ruth Has Been Promoted."[8] What an excellent choice of a word – *promotion*! This is a limited illustration, but when you are promoted from elementary school, it means you are leaving it forever; you are going on to something better – middle school! In work, just about every employee likes a promotion, especially if the benefits and working conditions are much better. For the believer, the best is yet to come; when we die, it is time for our *promotion*!

Lizzie Atwater once demonstrated great faith when facing death. Between 1830 and 1949 China was the largest Protestant mission field, but many of these brethren paid a great price. The largest massacre occurred in 1900, when a group called the Boxers waged war against believers. Nearly 200 missionary adults and children and 30,000 national Chinese Christians perished. Among them was missionary Lizzie Atwater who wrote her family on August 3, 1900, realizing her family was facing certain death. Here is her touching account.

> "Dear ones, I long for a sight of your dear faces, but I fear we shall not meet on earth. I am preparing for the end very quietly and calmly. The Lord is wonderfully near, and he will not fail me. I was very

restless and excited while there seemed a chance of life, but God has taken away that feeling. Now I just pray for grace to meet the terrible end bravely. The pain will soon be over, and oh the sweetness of the welcome above!

My little baby will go with me. I think God will give it to me in Heaven, and my dear mother will be so glad to see us. I cannot imagine the Savior's welcome. Oh, that will compensate for all these days of suspense. Dear ones, live near God and cling less closely to earth. There is no other way by which we can receive that peace from God which passeth understanding...."[9]

Twelve days later the Atwaters perished and they received their rich welcome into eternity. Believers can all be assured by God's own promise – to die is gain. We can be confident – our promotion is soon to come!

3. Death is a release.

As Job faced incredible physical suffering and the possibility of death, he exclaimed, *"If a man dies, will he live again? All the days of my hard service I will wait for my renewal to come."*[10] The word for *renewal* can also be translated *change* or *release.* In the Hebrew, it is a military word, used of one group of soldiers relieving another group. In the midst of our hard service, we will get a release, a well-deserved change! Roy Zuck commented, "Death, with its release from the burdens of this life, would be like an honorary discharge or changing of the guard."[11]

Probably for 90% of believers on this planet, just day-to-day living is quite difficult. Some of you may feel you are stuck in a difficult job, marriage, or economic situation. My advice is quite simple: HANG IN THERE! One day a release is coming! We will soon experience a wonderful change for the better!

At the end of his life, John Newton, author of "Amazing Grace," stated,

> More light, more love, more liberty. Hereafter, I hope, when I shut my eyes on the things of time, I shall open them in a better world. What a thing it is to live under the shadow of the wings of the Almighty![12]

The day is soon coming for all who are committed to Christ to be released – no more sorrows, no more disappointments, no more anxieties, no more bills to pay, no more cars to repair, no more house maintenance, and no more hassles common to life! HANG IN THERE! A RELEASE IS COMING!

4. Death is a mere transfer from one place to the next.

Writing from a prison cell and anticipating his death, the apostle Paul wrote,

> *I am torn between the two: I desire to depart and be with Christ, which is better by far; but it is more necessary for you that I remain in the body.*[13]

Death is a mere transfer from one place to the next. The Greek word used here for *depart* is full of meaning. In secular usage, this word meant "to loosen ropes in a ship, pull up the anchor and set sail," and "to loosen up tent pegs, to pick up one's tent and move on."[14]

So, when we die, we are just "setting sail to a better location," or we are just "moving our tents from here to there!" There is an ancient letter from 125 A.D. in which a Greek by the name of Aristides is writing to one of his friends about the new religion, Christianity. He is trying to explain the reason for its extraordinary success. Here is an interesting excerpt.

> "If any righteous man among the Christians passes from this world, they rejoice and offer thanks to God, and they escort his body with songs and thanksgiving as if he were setting out from one place to another nearby."[15]

The story is told of President John Quincy Adams, who, when he was eighty years old, was met by an old friend. This friend shook President Adams' trembling hand and said, "Good morning. How is John Quincy Adams today?" President Adams looked at him for a moment and then said,

> John Quincy Adams himself is quite well, sir, but the house in which he lives at present is becoming dilapidated. It is tottering upon its foundations. Time and the seasons have almost destroyed it. Its roof is worn out. Its walls are much shattered, and it crumbles with every wind. The old tenement is becoming almost uninhabitable, and I think that John Quincy Adams will have to move out of it soon. But he himself is well, sir, quite well![16]

Adams was saying he was ready to make the transition between the old and the new. So, what are we going to do when our earthly tent begins disintegrating? Are we going to live in a depressed state? Or, are we ready to "make a move" – to a much better locality in which there will be no disappointments!?

Especially in modern-day America, we can easily forget that this present world – with all its temporal joys – is not our home. The ancient men of faith whose stories are recorded in the Bible *admitted that they were aliens and strangers on earth... they were longing for a better country – a heavenly one.*[17] The Puritan teacher, Thomas Watson, wrote, "The world is but a great inn, where we are to stay a night or two, and be gone; what madness is it to set our heart upon our inn, as to forget our home."[18]

5. Death occurs in God's perfect timing.

This thought has been mentioned in an earlier chapter, but it is quite reassuring to know that we will not die before God's perfect time for us to "come home." There have been times, especially when traveling, that I have had thoughts about impending death or harm. Whenever that happens, I respond to these negative thoughts with the "sword of the Spirit," the word of God.

> *I will not die but live, and will proclaim what the LORD has done.*[19]

> *Be merciful to me, O LORD, for I am in distress; my eyes grow weak with sorrow, my soul and my body with grief. My life is consumed by anguish and my years by groaning; my strength fails because of my affliction, and my bones grow weak.... But I trust in you, O LORD; I say, "You are my God." My times are in your hands; deliver me from my enemies...*[20]

This ought to be our confession; "My times are in your hands..." Say it out loud right now...and whenever you think about possible, impending death.

In the Civil War, an officer once asked Stonewall Jackson after a battle, "How is it that you can keep so cool and appear to be so insensible to danger in such a storm of shell and bullets?" Jackson instantly became very somber in his attitude,

> "Captain, my religious belief teaches me to feel as safe in battle as in bed. God has fixed the time of my death. I do not concern myself about that, but to always be ready, no matter when it may overtake me. . . . That is the way all men should live, and then all would be equally brave."[21]

A. W. Tozer expressed the same confident attitude,

> "The man of true faith . . . cannot be torn from this earth one hour ahead of the time which God has appointed, and he cannot be detained on earth one moment after God is done with him here."[22]

Charles Spurgeon once said, "No believer dies an untimely death."[23] What reassurance if we believe this statement!

Why do some older folks still linger with us? Their health may be seriously deteriorating and they may say they earnestly want to "go home." Yet they linger. Even if it may not make sense to us, we must conclude they remain with us because it is *not yet God's time.* Our times are in his hands. We must realize that each of us will leave this earth in *God's* moment – not any sooner or later. It is recorded of King David,

> *For when David had served God's purpose in his own generation, he fell asleep; he was buried with his fathers and his body decayed.*[24]

Is this our attitude? "As long as I am on this earth, I want to *serve God's purpose.*" I personally pray that when I have accomplished all the works of God that he intends for me, that I too may *fall asleep* and be united with my Lord.

6. Death means we will soon have a complete "restoration job" of our bodies.

> *For when the trumpet sounds, the Christians who have died will be raised with transformed bodies. And then we who are living will be transformed so that we will never die. For our perishable earthly bodies must be transformed into heavenly bodies that will never die.*[25]

This is surely one of the most wonderful promises in all of Scripture! Men and women – if we do not have this great hope, when we hit our "senior years," we will likely be depressed persons!

Whenever we see an old house, car, or piece of furniture completely renovated, it is often quite impressive! In most cases, the renovated product is much better looking and more efficient than the original.

One day all believers are going to receive completely renovated bodies! No more aches and pains, no wrinkles, no malfunctions, no bruises and "age marks," and absolutely no disabilities! These bodies are described as *imperishable* and *heavenly*. What a future we can look forward to!

Heaven will be our ultimate "promise land." There will certainly be tasks to do in heaven, but no more laboring by the sweat of our brow. We will fully know the rest and joy of the Lord. We will hear the wonderful accolade from our Master, *"Well done, good and faithful servant....enter into the joy of your master!"*[26]

I sometimes have daydreams about the grand reunion we will have in heaven. Not only will we see our Lord Jesus, the patriarchs, and saints from all ages of church history, but we will also see our believing family members and friends. I have sometimes imagined what it will be like to see my parents and other relatives – looking young and healthy, laughing, and expressing life in all its fullness!

D. L. Moody believed that death would be the gateway to experiencing a brand new body and all the benefits of heaven.

> Someday you will read in the paper that D.L. Moody of Northfield is dead. Don't you believe a word of it. At that moment I shall be more alive than I am now. I shall have gone higher, that is all – out of this clay tenement into a house that is immortal, a body that sin cannot touch, that sin cannot taint, a body fashioned into his glorious body. I was born in the flesh in 1837; I was born of the Spirit in 1856. That

which is born of the flesh may die; that which is born of the Spirit will live forever.[27]

7. Death ushers us into the presence of God.

Therefore we are always confident and know that as long as we are at home in the body we are away from the Lord. We live by faith, not by sight. We are confident, I say, and would prefer to be away from the body and at home with the Lord.[28]

Dear friends, now we are children of God, and what we will be has not yet been made known. But we know that when he appears, we shall be like him, for we shall see him as he is. Everyone who has this hope in him purifies himself, just as he is pure.[29]

The greatest blessing we will ever experience is to see our Lord and Savior Jesus – face-to-face. I personally think he's going to have a grin on his face when we see him! This encounter will bring the ultimate satisfaction to our longing hearts. The psalmist said,

But as for me, my contentment is not in wealth but in seeing you and knowing all is well between us. And when I awake in heaven, I will be fully satisfied, for I will see you face-to-face.[30]

Just think about being a permanent resident of heaven – and especially being in the presence of the Lord Jesus himself, whose loving fellowship we will enjoy forever. The famous poet, John Milton, in his final words declared, "Death is the great key that opens the palace of eternity."[31]

Some believe a false doctrine of "soul sleep" – that when we die, our souls sleep until the final resurrection. However, when the Bible talks about "sleeping" it is talking about our *physical* bodies, not our souls. Scripture is clear: *to be absent from the body is to be present with the Lord.* There can be no greater joy than this!

So, Believers Have No Need To Fear!

Sometimes, we find ourselves facing the fear of death. This often happens when we receive a serious medical diagnosis or it may happen when we have a close call, like a car accident. Some have just a general sense of foreboding and others are even tormented by an unusual fear – a phobia of death.

Hans Christian Andersen, the famous author of such fairy tales as "The Emperor's New Clothes" and "The Ugly Duckling," apparently had a phobia of dying. His fear of dying in a fire was so great that he packed a rope in his suitcase when he traveled in order to escape from a window. He was especially terrified of being buried alive. As a result, he often left a hand-written note on his bedside table stating, "I only appear to be dead." Evidently this man was tormented by this fear until he finally succumbed to cancer in 1875.[32]

The Bible calls death an "enemy"[33] but Jesus has overcome this enemy. There is good news today for any who might have a fear of death – Jesus died to free you from any fear of death!

> *Because God's children are human beings – made of flesh and blood – Jesus also became flesh and blood by being born in human form. For only as a human being could he die, and only by dying could he break the power of the Devil, who had the power of death. Only in this way could he deliver those who have lived all their lives as slaves to the fear of dying.*[34]

John and Betty Stam were missionaries with the China Inland Mission in the 1930's. Only two years after arriving they misjudged the safety of the area and found their lives in grave danger of the communists. They soon realized death was imminent. Although they had every reason to fear for their lives, a poem written by another missionary sustained them until the very end in December 1934. This godly couple was faithful, even to death.

AFRAID? OF WHAT?

Afraid? Of What?
To feel the spirit's glad release?
To pass from pain to perfect peace,
The strife and strain of life to cease?
Afraid – of that?

Afraid? Of What?
Afraid to see the Savior's face
To hear his welcome, and to trace
The glory gleam from wounds of grace?
Afraid – of that?

Afraid? Of What?
A flash, a crash, a pierced heart;
Darkness, light, O Heaven's art!
A wound of His a counterpart?
Afraid – of that?

Afraid? Of What?
To do by death what life could not –
Baptized with blood a stony plot,
Till souls shall blossom from the spot?
Afraid – of that?[35]

The closer we get to death, the more we can rejoice. Believers need not fear; we have a *lot* to look forward to! If tempted to fear, we can always take courage – the Lord will be our light to guide us in "stormy times" and our Good Shepherd to lead us – even through the darkest valleys.

The LORD is my light and my salvation – whom shall I fear? The LORD is the stronghold of my life – of whom shall I be afraid?
When evil men advance against me to devour my flesh, when my enemies and my foes attack me, they will stumble and fall.
Though an army besiege me, my heart will not fear; though war break out against me, even then will I be confident.
One thing I ask of the LORD, this is what I seek: that I may dwell in the house of the LORD all the days of my life, to gaze upon the beauty of the LORD and to seek him in his temple. (Psalm 27:1-4)

CHAPTER TEN

LEAVING A LASTING LEGACY

What we have heard and known, what our fathers have told us.
We will not hide them from their children; we will tell the next generation the praiseworthy deeds of the LORD, his power, and the wonders he has done...
so the next generation would know them, even the children yet to be born, and they in turn would tell their children.
Then they would put their trust in God and would not forget his deeds but would keep his commands.
(Psalm 78:3-7)

One day when we breathe our last and our bodies are buried in the grave, what will people remember about us? In the years that follow our death, what will we have passed on to the next generation? What legacy will we leave behind? By *legacy*, we use Webster's definition, "Anything handed down from the past, as from an ancestor or predecessor."[1] Scripture says, *A good man leaves an inheritance for his children's children.*[2]

The word *inheritance* is similar to *legacy*. We tend to think of "inheritance" as property or money left to descendants through a deceased person's will. In biblical understanding, however, the word "inheritance" includes more than mere material things. It can also include gifts from our character, our words, our faith, and our contribution to God's kingdom.

In this chapter we will look at various aspects of leaving a lasting legacy.

The Importance of Leaving a Written Will

Why is it that four out of five people do not prepare a written will? Probably it is because we tend to avoid the unpleasant reality of our inevitable death! I remember when my wife and I finally had a will made, I felt a little strange – like maybe something bad would happen now!

When King Hezekiah was facing a sickness that would lead to death, the prophet Isaiah brought this message, "This is what the LORD says: Put your house in order, because you are going to die…"[3] How about us – is our "house in order"? If we were to die right now, would our important papers be found in "good order?" Have we left any instructions or final words for our family and friends? We must not neglect our families – even after we die.

God has placed a prioritry on preparing for the future. One instruction given to his people stated,

> *If a man dies and leaves no son, turn his inheritance over to his daughter. If he has no daughter, give his inheritance to his brothers. If he has no brothers, give his inheritance to his father's brothers. If his father had no brothers, give his inheritance to the nearest relative in his clan, that he may possess it. This is to be a legal requirement for the Israelites, as the LORD commanded Moses.*[4]

Wills are especially important if children are involved. If a set of parents die without a will, then it is left to the state as to where to place the children. A will is also important because any money or property left may bless descendants or Christian organizations that are so designated. Please carefully consider preparing a will if you have not yet done so.

Leaving a Legacy of Written Words

In addition to leaving a will, have you considered writing down some final thoughts to leave with family and friends? The Bible says, *Wisdom* is *good with an inheritance... For wisdom* is *a defense* as *money* is *a defense.... wisdom gives life to those who have it.*[5] Some years ago, when my sons were still young, I wrote out a two page letter to my wife and sons – some words of wisdom and encouragement – in case I would ever pass away earlier than expected. I attached copies to both copies of wills we have, so they could easily be found. Since then, I have twice updated my letter. It takes some fortitude to write such a letter as this, because you will likely feel uncomfortable like I did while doing it! However, final words are often not only an encouragement to one's family, but may also bless others who later read or hear them.

SOME EXAMPLES OF FINAL WORDS[6]

The following are examples of final words recorded from various famous people just before they died. Some of these words will certainly encourage us – now many years after they died. Recorded words can have ongoing power!

- **Bernard of Clairvaux:** "I beg you, dearest brethren, love one another."

- **William Carey:** "When I am gone, speak less of Dr. Carey and more of Dr. Carey's Savior."

- **G. K. Chesterton:** "The issue is now clear. It is between light and darkness and everyone must choose his side."

- **King David:** "...When one rules over men in righteousness, when he rules in the fear of God, he is like the light of morning at sunrise on a cloudless morning, like the brightness after rain that brings the grass from the earth…" (2 Sam. 23:1-4)

- **Matthew Henry:** "You have been used to take notice of the sayings of dying men. This is mine: that a life spent in the service of God, and communion with him, is the most comfortable and pleasant life that anyone can live in this world."

- **Martin Luther: "**God so loved the world, that he gave his only begotten Son, that whosoever believeth in him should not perish, but have everlasting life." [Repeated three times.]

- **D. L. Moody:** "Earth is receding; heaven is approaching. This is my crowning day!"

- **John Wesley:** "The best of all is, God is with us. Farewell!"

What inspiring final words – words of wisdom even to our generation! What words might we also leave that would be a blessing to those left behind?

Leaving a Legacy of Good Memories

Before my mother died, we talked much about our ancestors. I have never been big on genealogies and saving family memorabilia, but I wanted to clarify some family history and be able to recall some aspects of my mother's Christian faith. With my help, we made a set of photo scrapbooks – one for each of her five sons – with photos and dates of the last four generations of ancestors – on each side of the family. These scrapbooks will always be a remembrance of our forefathers.

My mother also collected different devotional thoughts she had written herself or gleaned from others, a story she had written as a young girl, and some family memories, like when she met my dad. These were assembled into five notebooks, with a front cover, "Memories of Mom."

Family memories are a legacy we can pass on. This is why, if possible, we ought to invest time with grandchildren. Some stories can be told to them that may be remembered. Collectible items can be explained and history shared. When certain questions are asked, we can share aspects of our faith and pray blessings upon them. We can also add to memories of "good times" at Grandma's house. When our three grandsons visit us, we get quite involved. I think they have yet to be bored when they visit here! We have a zip-line in the backyard, a "speedway" in the basement, and once even bought three baby ducks to raise for a while. Recently, despite our aches and pains, we took them to a large indoor waterpark and had a blast! While we are physically able, we ought to be very active with our grandkids – making memories that will last a lifetime.

Leaving a Legacy of a Life Well Lived

How often have you been to a memorial service and heard a preacher extol all the *possessions* the man owned?

> "We are here to remember the life of our dearly departed Bob Smith. Bob was an amazing man of much wealth. He owned three houses and had a fleet of six cars. His bank accounts were in the millions. He flew his own jet and was on top of the latest technology. When the latest computer, TV, or phone was on the market, Bob would be the first in town to own the coveted item. We all have happy memories of Bob and his possessions."

That kind of eulogy would be absurd, wouldn't it? At funerals, most of the words spoken usually deal with the deceased man's *life* and his *character*. For example,

> "Those who knew Bob Smith were quick to say that he was a most kind and gracious man. We all remember the service projects he contributed to our town and how he especially had a compassionate heart for the needy. Bob loved his family deeply and was not an absentee dad. His wife said he was a most thoughtful person and always quick to help others…"

If your wife and children were to share some thoughts at your funeral, what do you think they would say? What qualities would they remember and be quick to applaud in your life? Would they talk about your sincere faith, self-denying love, and your concern and care for others? Or, would their only thoughts be like these, "He liked to enjoy himself;" "He was a successful businessman;" or "He provided well." Sadly, I have conducted funerals where such expressions were the best that family members could come up with.

Charles Colson was influenced much by the life of William Wilberforce. Wilberforce was the man who campaigned for two decades against slavery in the British Parliament, finally passing a bill to abolish the slave trade in 1807. Then, after many more years of labor, on his deathbed in 1883, Wilberforce received news that slavery itself had been abolished throughout the empire.

Colson decided to visit the hometown of Wilberforce and locate any memorable sites or monuments to this great man. In the town of Clapham, Wilberforce's homeplace was no longer standing. When asked what monuments were there to remember his hero, Colson was directed to the Anglican church in which Wilberforce preached. As they entered, the rector proudly pointed to a stained glass window. Colson squinted in the dark room to make out what it was, and finally he saw a small profile of Wilberforce in a square no wider than ten inches in the center of one window. Beneath the window was a shelf with some brochures entitled, "Clapham Sect Information."

Needless to say, Colson was extremely disappointed by such a little memorial. As he left the place, however, God gave him a powerful insight.

> In my mind's eye I saw a long line of slaves in tattered loincloths, walking across the green with their chains falling off. *Of course*, I thought to myself, *Of course – that's it. Wilberforce's legacy is not in monuments or churches or stained-glass windows. It's in lives set free. The black men and women who are no longer subject to slavery are the living monuments of William Wilberforce and his work. Generations of people can thank Wilberforce for changing their destinies.*[7]

So, the best legacy is not the things or memorials we leave behind, but *a life well lived.* People will likely cherish fond memories of any man or woman whose character was Christ-like and whose selfless deeds still bear fruit today.

Leaving a Legacy of Faith

The best legacy we can pass on to our children and others is a genuine faith in Jesus Christ. If my sons remember anything about me, I hope the first thing that comes to their mind was, "Dad was a man who loved the Lord and sought to do his will." John McElroy said,

> What we leave behind as a legacy reveals our priorities. It shows how we want to be remembered. It unveils whether we pointed to Jesus or us. It is the testimony of God's work in our lives; the spiritual inheritance or baton that we leave to others.[8]

We see an example of this "passed-on-faith" in Timothy's grandmother and mother. Many Bible commentators believe that Timothy's father was likely a Greek and a non-believer. The father's faith is never mentioned, but the spiritual contributions of the grandmother and mother are mentioned.

> *I have been reminded of your sincere faith, which first lived in your grandmother Lois and in your mother Eunice and, I am persuaded, now lives in you also.*[9]

Grandparents should never underestimate the power of their faith – lived out and verbally shared with their children and grandchildren. Like many busy women, Lois may have never thought she was making much contribution to God's work, yet her faith was passed on to her grandson, Timothy, who was one of the outstanding leaders in the early church. We also have two letters in our Bible that are addressed to Timothy by Paul. Grandparents, take heart, and let your light shine! The spiritual seeds you are planting may reap quite a harvest one day!

Many of us are familiar with the books written by Charles Dickens, like *David Copperfield, A Tale of Two Cities,* and his great classic, *A Christmas Carol*. In his last days, he wrote these words,

> "I commit my soul to the mercy of God, through our Lord and Savior Jesus Christ, and I exhort my dear children humbly to try and guide themselves by the teaching of the New Testament."

Patrick Henry, like many other American Revolutionary leaders, paid a dear price financially for his pursuit of liberty. Apparently he had little to leave his family, but his will emphasized something much better than money or property.

> "This is all the inheritance I can give to my dear family. The religion of Christ can give them [an inheritance] which will make them rich indeed."[10]

As we have mentioned, leaving our family some financial means, is a good thing. But are we leaving them *an inheritance that can never perish, spoil or fade*?[11] Let us not neglect the most important legacy we can pass on – a personal knowledge of Christ and a genuine faith worth imitating.

CHAPTER ELEVEN

RESISTING THE RETIREMENT MENTALITY

A former teacher recently graduated from a university in Ghana – at the age of ninety-nine! World War II veteran, Akasease Kofi Boakye Yiadom, enrolled at Presbyterian University's business school at the age of ninety-six. "Education has no end," he told CNN. "As long as your brain can work alright, if you go to school you can learn."

What a great attitude! Today, especially in America, there is an emphasis on working so many years and then finally "retiring" – when we draw some government income, spend our savings, and *"Take life easy; eat, drink and be merry."*[1] Such persons think, "After sixty-five, I'm going to be through with work and will finally be able to take it easy. I am going to get what I deserve and enjoy myself, travel, and just have fun."

The Bible is not against our planning for the future or enjoying life. Indeed, some of us will end our work careers as we enter our older years; however, if Jesus Christ is Lord, should we not desire to live for the Master and do his will until the day we die?

John Piper encourages us to resist the "retirement mentality."

> Getting old to the glory of God means resolutely resisting the typical American dream of retirement. It means being so satisfied with all that God promises

> to be for us in Christ that we are set free from the cravings that create so much emptiness and uselessness in retirement. Instead, knowing that we have an infinitely satisfying and everlasting inheritance in God just over the horizon of life makes us zealous in our few remaining years here to spend ourselves in the sacrifices of love, not the accumulation of comforts. . . Live dangerously for the One who loved you and died for you in his thirties. Don't throw your life away on the American dream of retirement.[2]

On a similar note, Dr. Robert Lightner, a former professor at Dallas Theological Seminary, stated, "Keep busy as long as you can. Keep involved. Do not sit, soak, and sour!"[3]

I fully realize some older folks suffer physical afflictions that severely limit their mobility and even their mental capability. I am not addressing those who are suffering like this and must – out of necessity – restrain their activity. Rather, I am talking about those who "grow old before their time," and those who are still quite capable, but are retreating from God-honoring work.

"Give me Another Mountain!"

I appreciate the spirit of those who have not bought into the "retirement mentality." May we follow the examples of those great souls who seemed always ready for more action in this present life and were willing to live out their lives for the glory of God.

- **Caleb** had a long "career" in serving the Lord. It was Caleb and Joshua who were among the spies going into the land of Canaan and the only two who were optimistic about conquering the land. *"We should go up and take possession of the land, for we can certainly do it.... The Lord is with* *us!"*[4] Many years later, at the age of eighty-five, Caleb was still active. When dividing up the land, Caleb did not ask for a rocking chair; he said, "*Now therefore, give me this mountain ... the Anakim were there... the cities were great and fortified. It may be that the Lord will be with me, and I shall be able to drive them out as the Lord said."*[5] As we age, may we have this same heart attitude that Caleb had, "Lord, give me another mountain! I'm ready for another project! I'll fight another battle!"

- **Anna** was one of the few privileged persons to see the baby Jesus. This prophetess and widow was eighty-four, but it is recorded that *she never left the temple but worshiped night and day, fasting and praying... she was looking forward to the redemption of Jerusalem.*[6] Here this older lady, likely limited in body, was still being active in what she *could* do, and certainly not shrinking back from her devotion to God.

- **Billy Graham** apparently rarely gets agitated. One close friend, as Graham approached his eightieth birthday, commented that he had only seen him get agitated in one situation – when some people started encouraging him to retire and spend more time writing. Graham replied, "No, my call is to preach the gospel, and I will do that as long as God gives me the breath to preach."[7]

- **Andrew Murray** and his wife were at a conference and she said, "I think we ought to go home now, we are getting old." He replied, "Speak for yourself . . . . I'm not ready to die . . . . There is much to be done still!"[8] One of his family members wrote this about him:

> Father speaks very quietly now, with very little exertion, but with great spiritual power. It seems like a voice on the verge of eternity, of one just ready to go on living as long as God wills. Glad to live to deliver God's messages, but he talks little and spares all his strength for work, yet

> he was never more bright and joyous in his whole life, so restful and peaceful. The world and its interests are diminishing; God's kingdom and its interests absorb his thoughts and heart.[9]

- **John Wesley** served Christ quite actively even late in life. As an older man he was still traveling countless miles on horseback, writing extensively, and preaching almost daily. On his eighty-fifth birthday (June 28, 1788), he wrote in his journal,

> And what cause have I to praise God, as for a thousand spiritual blessings, so for bodily blessings also! How little have I suffered yet by 'the rush of numerous years!' It is true, I am not so agile as I was in times past. I do not run or walk so fast as I did; my sight is a little decayed; my left eye is grown dim, and hardly serves me to read. . . I find likewise some decay in my memory, with regard to names and things lately passed; but not at all with regard to what I have read or heard, twenty, forty, or sixty years ago . . . nor do I feel any such thing as weariness, either in traveling or preaching: And I am not conscious of any decay in writing sermons; which I do as readily, and I believe as correctly, as ever.
>
> To what cause can I impute this, that I am as I am? First, doubtless, to the power of God, fitting me for the work to which I am called, as long as He pleases to continue me therein; and, next, subordinately to this, to the prayers of his children.[10]

- **Earl Seamands** faithfully served as a missionary in India for thirty-seven years and retired in 1957 at the age of sixty-five. He was a man sold out to Jesus. "If you're going to be a Christian," he once said, "be a Christian to your fingertips."[11] A few years before his retirement, Seamands wrote,

> It was during our last furlough as we listened on the radio to General Douglas McArthur's masterful farewell address before the American Congress. Rising to a grand finale, he quoted the well-known military slogan, "Old soldiers never die, they just fade away!" The Holy Spirit whispered, "*That's not for you!* As an old soldier of the cross, don't you just *fade away*; you keep on *firing away*!" I responded, "Lord, that's a deal. I will, provided you inspire the saints to bring up the ammunition!"[12]

Indeed, Seamands' next twenty-seven years would be the most fruitful years of his life. He would make twelve more yearly "shuttle service missions" to India – each one usually three months in length. He spoke in public frequently and took any opportunities to share Christ one-on-one. He raised money and because he was an engineer by profession, he helped in constructing 175 church buildings. This old saint apparently "kept firing away" – until he died at age ninety-two!

Old Age Can Be Quite Productive!

We tend to think most significant work occurs in the prime of one's life. But for many individuals, some of their greatest contributions occurred later in life. Consider a few examples.

- Moses, at eighty, obeyed God's commission to deliver His people from Egypt (Ex. 7:7).
- Miriam, at eighty-three, was still joyfully praising God (Ex. 15:20).

- Joshua, at an old age, was still a builder (Josh. 19:50).
- Daniel, in his eighties, wrote some of the most detailed prophecies in the Bible (Dan. 10-12).
- Paul, describing himself as "an old man" (Phm. 9) was still writing Scripture and encouraging reconciliation between a slave and his master.
- John the apostle, possibly in his nineties (according to commentators), received and wrote *The Revelation.*
- Noah Webster, at seventy, wrote his monumental dictionary.
- Benjamin Franklin, at eighty-one, helped frame the Constitution.
- William Gladstone, at eighty-three, became Prime Minister of England.
- Grandma Moses did many paintings when she was in her nineties.
- Former President George H. W. Bush celebrated his eighty-fifth birthday by making a tandem skydiving jump. He said, "Just because you're an old guy, you don't have to sit around. . . Get out and do something. Get out and enjoy life!"
- Commodore Vanderbilt, when well past seventy, built most of his railroads.
- John Glenn, at seventy-five, returned to space.
- Michelangelo, in his eighties, was still producing masterpieces.
- George Bernard Shaw began his playwriting career in his fifties and worked into his nineties.
- James Cash Penney founder of "The Golden Rule Stores" – later to become J. C. Penney stores – wrote spiritual memoirs based on his business experiences well into his eighties.
- Hudson Taylor, at sixty-nine, was still vigorously working in the mission field, opening up new territories in Indochina.
- George Mueller, at seventy, started a new phase of missionary work abroad. During the next twenty years

he preached to more than three million people in forty-two countries of the world.

Who knows what good things – either small or large – might still come from us in our latter years? It might even be the most productive time of our life!

What Will Be Our Attitude in Older Age: Stay Active While We Can... or Corrode?

Helen Turner has amazed many of the people who know her. When I first met Helen, she was sixty-five years old, and had begun teaching an elementary class (full time) at our Christian school. She previously had custody of a great grandchild since he was eighteen months old. In addition, she did tax work on the side and cared for a few elderly patients! Some of us would just shake our heads whenever we considered her tireless energy and joyful disposition in doing her work.

As I am writing this, Helen is now seventy-eight years old. She has cut back her teaching role to substitute teaching but is working for a caretaker agency at least thirty hours a week and still does some tax work. When I asked her what she liked to do for recreation she mentioned fishing and white-water rafting!

When I asked if there was any advice she could give for staying active and optimistic about life, she mentioned two things: (1) get around children when you can, and (2) whenever you have physical setbacks, don't give up – look to the Lord for help and keep on going!

I say, "Lord, give us the energy and spirit of Helen!"

If we are not staying active and outwardly focused – on the Lord and others – we may tend to become more self-occupied the older we get. We will talk excessively about our aches and pains and our attention will be absorbed by our own comfort and happiness.

Paul Tournier, a Swiss psychologist and medical doctor, in his book *Learn to Grow Old,* advised patients to stay active *while they were able.* He observed,

> Lots of retired people are bored because they do not know what to do with their enforced liberty! For lack of imagination, lack of habit, lack of training, they let themselves go, and take no interest in anything. They retire into a shell of boredom, and in the end any renewal becomes impossible, and they become a burden to others. But the germ of this passivity has been there within them for years. They have not realized it, because the routine of work and social life has covered up the void in their personal lives. So many people – including young people – claim liberty, and they have little idea of what to do with it when they get it, because they have not been prepared for it.[13]

Many people who retire soon discover that the "life of leisure" wasn't all they hoped it would be. Charles Colson, in his excellent book, *The Good Life,* shared the following insight.

> I have seen how debilitating the lack of stimulating work can be. One friend, a person of some accomplishment, stopped practicing law early in life so that he could enjoy traveling with his wife and visiting their four homes. He had everything the American dream tells us we should live for, but he had nothing significant to do. Over a ten-year period I watched him deteriorate mentally, emotionally, and physically. I really believe the stress of trying to appear normal in a circumstance where he had nothing to give, nothing to fulfill his desire for significance, became draining to the point of destruction. When people are idle, they lack purpose and begin to corrode like an unused piece of

equipment....Some senior citizens have discovered that the goal of life is not leisure but to keep working, sometimes into their seventies, eighties, and nineties.[14]

A good example of an active senior citizen is S. S. Borum, who at the age of ninety-six was preaching twice a month at a nursing home, visiting folks in hospitals regularly, and sharing Christ one-on-one with people whenever he sensed an open door. He said he did not believe in retirement, but only in "changing gears." He encourages other seniors to be active in serving Christ, He said, "Don't let up....Forget yourself and keep on going as the Lord leads you."[15]

George Jones, the famous country singer, at the age of sixty-two, wrote a humorous song, "I Don't Need Your Rockin' Chair!" These lyrics have occasionally come to my mind and encouraged me to keep "pressing on" when I'm feeling weary. Our prayer ought to be, "Lord, help me physically, mentally, and spiritually stay active! Keep me from the 'rockin' chair' mentality!"

What Will We Do NOW?

It is a good thing to be productive in this present life as long as we are able. We are confident of our future hope of heaven, but as far as living – our focus must be on NOW. Oswald Chambers once said, "*Always now* is the secret of the Christian life."[16] This idea is confirmed by Scripture, *The grace of God...teaches us...to live here and now, responsible, honorable, and God fearing lives.*[17] So, living *here and now* is commendable and quite possible – by the grace of God. John Ortberg has encouraged this mentality.

I believe that the greatest moment of your life is this moment right here. This tick of the clock. This beat of your heart.

The greatest moment of your life is *now*.

Not because it's pleasant or happy or easy, but because this moment is the only moment you've got. Every past moment is irretrievably gone. It's never coming back. If you live there, you lose your life.

And the future is always out there somewhere. You can spend an eternity waiting for tomorrow, or worrying about tomorrow. If you live there, you likewise will lose your life.

This moment is God's irreplaceable gift to you. Most of all, this is the moment that matters because this moment is where God is. If you are going to be with God at all, you must be with him now - in this moment.

That is why the psalmist says, "This is the day the Lord has made; let us rejoice and be glad in it." That is why the prophet says God's mercies never fail because "they are new every morning." That is why the apostle Paul says, "Be very careful, then, how you live - not as unwise but as wise, making the most of every opportunity."

I believe this can be the greatest moment of your life because this moment is the place where you can meet God. In fact, this moment is the only place where you can meet God.[18]

Sometimes, we fail to act in the present because we are waiting for ideal conditions in the future. I read of one man who worked so hard he never had time to take trips and enjoy vacation time with his family. Finally, in his mid-sixties, his wife received her long-awaited promise. He would retire and now they could do many of the exciting things they had always dreamed about. He did retire...and three weeks later he died of a heart attack. How sad.

Some years ago, Ann Wells wrote an article in the *Los Angeles Times* of another sad situation.

> My brother-in-law opened the bottom drawer of my sister's bureau and lifted out a tissue-wrapped package, "This," he said, "is not a slip. This is lingerie." He discarded the tissue and handed me the slip. It was exquisite: silk, handmade and trimmed with a cobweb of lace. The price tag with an astronomical figure on it was still attached.
>
> "Jan bought this the first time we went to New York, at least eight or nine years ago. She never wore it. She was saving it for a special occasion. Well, I guess this is the occasion."
>
> He took the slip from me and put it on the bed with the other clothes we were taking to the mortician. His hands lingered on the soft material for a moment, then he slammed the drawer shut and turned to me.
>
> "Don't ever save anything for a special occasion. Every day you're alive is a special occasion."[19]

Profound words indeed: *Every day you're alive is a special occasion.* How often have we used the words, "someday..." or "one of these days..."? May we not fail to live in the *now* as we live out our remaining years.

How Do You Want To Spend Your Remaining Years?

What do you think about the remaining years of your life? How do you want to spend them – actively or passively? I have been impressed with the attitude of three elderly pastors. Charles Swindoll, a man who has served Christ for five decades, was recently asked, "How do you want to spend the remainder of your years?" He replied,

> I want to preach till the last breath in my lungs runs out. Nothing is more bothersome to me than retiring. Weird things happen when you disengage; first you get negative, then you start telling people about your latest surgeries, and eventually you lose touch. I want to stay in touch.[20]

Our second active example is a friend of Bo Barredo, named "Papa Ramon." Barredo, the president of Advancing Native Missions, shared this story about his dear friend.

> In 1988, during one of my travels visiting small islands in central Philippines, I was accompanied by an eighty-six year old seminary-trained Filipino missionary leader, "Papa Ramon" Cenit. We were in outrigger boats going to several very tiny islands that disappear during high tide! The inhabitants live in houses on stilts. Local missionaries like Papa Ramon would approach these islands during high tide and drop anchor in the middle of clumps of houses. The people were "a captive audience" for the sharing of the Gospel through battery-powered megaphones – they had nowhere to go!
>
> With concern, I asked Papa Ramon why didn't he just stay home and leave this type of hard evangelistic endeavor to his younger workers. His response? *"Brother Bo, I ask the Lord each day to give me the strength to visit these isolated places to look for lost souls. Who knows that the Lord will grant this humble servant of His the honor of bringing to His throne the last soul He is waiting for? Then, even so, He shall come."*[21]

Our third example of a man staying active for Christ until the end is E. Stanley Jones, a Methodist missionary and evangelist, who spent over fifty years in India. He spoke to millions of people, met with presidents and prime ministers, and led countless people to Christ.

> When he was seventy years old, God spoke to his heart, "I'm giving you the best ten years of your life - the next ten ahead." Jones added, "Two of them have passed and they have literally been the best two years of my life. Eight to go! . . . Practically all my question marks have now been straightened out into dancing exclamation marks!"[22]

What an attitude! - Can we say to the Lord - "Lord, I want the next ten years of my life to be the best years yet!"

When Jones was eighty-three, he suffered a serious stroke that left him without speech or physical mobility. Before he died, he was able to mutter through paralyzed lips the words for one more book. One excerpt,

> There are scars on my faith, but underneath those scars there are no doubts....I am eighty-three and I'm more excited today about being a Christian than I was at eighteen when I first put my feet to the way.[23]

Brethren - especially you who are my age (sixty) or beyond - can this be our attitude as well? Are we as "excited about being a Christian" right now more than ever? Will we just settle back and enjoy the self-indulged "good life" in the years to come, or will we say with Caleb, "Lord, give me another mountain"?!

CHAPTER TWELVE

FINISHING OUR RACE WELL

On Oct. 20, 1968, a dramatic moment took place at the Mexico City Olympics. As the last of the marathon runners stumbled across the finish line, a few thousand spectators remained in the almost-dark Olympic Stadium. Suddenly, the wail of police sirens ripped the air. As all eyes turned to the gate, a lone runner wearing the colors of Tanzania, Africa, staggered into the stadium. John Stephen Akhwari was the last contestant to finish the 26 mile contest. He had injured his leg in a fall and entered the track bloodied and crudely bandaged. While he hobbled the final, lonely lap, spectators rose and applauded him as if he had won.

After the race, someone asked Akhwari why he had refused to quit. "My country did not send me to Mexico City to start the race," he replied simply. "They sent me to finish it."

JOHN STEPHEN AKHWARI

In an athletic race, the end is the most important thing. This is also true in the race of life. Scripture says, *The end of a matter is better than its beginning...* [1]

Several Scriptures compare the Christian life to running a race.

> *Brothers, I do not consider myself yet to have taken hold of it. But one thing I do: Forgetting what is behind and straining toward what is ahead, I press on toward the goal to win the prize for which God has called me heavenward in Christ Jesus.*[2]

> *Therefore, since we are surrounded by such a great cloud of witnesses, let us throw off everything that hinders and the sin that so easily entangles, and let us run with perseverance the race marked out for us. Let us fix our eyes on Jesus, the author and perfecter of our faith, who for the joy set before him endured the cross, scorning its shame, and sat down at the right hand of the throne of God.*[3]

Our life can be compared to a long-distance race, not a sprint. We are in this race for the "long-haul."

We are not in competition with each other; our race is individual. Our speed or place at the finish line will not matter in this race. Handicapped runners will run a slower-paced race. The important thing is for each of us to *finish.*

We are not looking at each other; our eyes are fixed *on Jesus.* We are to run our particular race – *the race marked out for us.*

Athletes cannot be haphazard and expect to finish their race well. A successful athlete must have much discipline. *Everyone who competes in the games goes into strict training. They do it to get a crown that will not last; but we do it to get a crown that will last forever.*[4] If we are to be successful Christians, we will need to excel in spiritual disciplines, like prayer, study of the Word, guarding the lusts of the flesh, and so on. This is not to imply we rely on our own strength and ability. No, Jesus is the *author and perfecter of our faith.*

Any successful athlete will say it takes *perseverance* to finish well. This truth is also confirmed in Scripture: *Let us run with* perseverance *the race marked out for us.*[5] *It is the one who has* endured *to the end who will be saved.*[6] In the parable of "The Sower and the Seed," only one out of four types of soil receive the seed and produce good fruit. What kind of soil is good and fruitful? *"The seed on good soil stands for those with a noble and good heart, who hear the word, retain it, and by* persevering *produce a crop."*[7]

From this parable, we can sadly conclude that the majority of people who show an interest in Christ will *not* continue on the journey. Dr. Howard Henricks did a study and discovered the following:

- 2,930 individuals are mentioned in the Bible.
- We know details of about 100 of these individuals.
- Of those 100, only one-third of them finished well.[8]

In another study, a few years ago Dr. Robert Clinton, Associate Professor of Leadership at the School of World Mission, Fuller Theological Seminary, did extensive research on the lives of over six hundred leaders – both past and present. He concluded that most leaders do NOT finish well. He also observed that those who finished well seemed to share some common characteristics.

1. They could relate present circumstances to the long-range view. They could see the broader view of life and ministry.
2. They enjoyed intimacy with Christ and experienced repeated times of inner renewal.
3. They were disciplined in important areas of life.
4. They maintained a positive learning attitude all their lives.
5. They had a network of meaningful relationships and several important mentors during their lifetime.[9]

These two studies are quite sobering. What about you and me? Will we be in that select company of those who *finish* well? Will we keep *enduring* despite all obstacles? Are we committed to *persevere* to the very end?

We have many good examples to follow of those who have finished well.

The Example of the Priest, Samuel

Samuel was one of the greatest leaders in the history of Israel. It is recorded that w*hen Samuel grew old, he appointed his sons as judges for Israel.*[10] Samuel's sons, however, did not walk in the ways of the Lord and Israel persisted in wanting a king. God was displeased, but he allowed Israel to have what they wanted. Samuel graciously anointed the new king, Saul, and then he stepped aside. The old man Samuel, however, did not just retire and do nothing. He stated,

> *As for me, far be it from me that I should sin against the LORD by failing to pray for you. And I will teach you the way that is good and right. But be sure to fear the LORD and serve him faithfully with all your heart; consider what great things he has done for you.*[11]

Even as an old man, Samuel continued in two vital ministries – teaching younger men the ways of God and engaging in intercessory prayer. Dr. V. Raymond Edman, a past president of Wheaton College, said,

> In my opinion, Samuel did more for Israel in the days of retirement than in all the long years of active and conspicuous service. He prayed for people and their new king in days that were darker and more difficult than any they had known under Samuel's

administration...The Divine Record states succinctly: "Moses and Aaron were among his priests and Samuel was among them that call upon his name, they called upon the Lord, and he answered them."[12]

The Example of the Evangelist, Bill Bright

Bill Bright has been one of the most influential Christians in recent history. A former businessman, Bill, along with his wife, Vonette, began Campus Crusade For Christ on the UCLA campus in 1951. Now, sixty years later, Campus Crusade is active in over 190 countries with 25,000 staff members and 500,000 trained volunteers, sharing their faith in Christ. They are active on over a thousand college campuses. Over two-and-a-half billion copies of *The Four Spiritual Laws* have been distributed. The *JESUS* film project, has been seen by an estimated five billion people. It is hard to fathom all that Bill Bright has contributed for the cause of Christ.

In the year 2000, Bright was told by his doctors that he had pulmonary fibrosis and would likely die within a couple years. His attitude was quite remarkable in the remaining three years of life. Although Bright was constantly on oxygen and limited physically, he pressed on in faith. He certainly finished his race well. His book, *The Journey Home: Finishing With Joy*, was published in 2003 – the year he died. Here are a few of his encouraging comments.

> Many feel that their work is finished, that there is nothing left to be accomplished. Some feel that there is no future for themselves. Many feel that they are just waiting to die....
>
> I never intended retirement, and I am so grateful to God that He has kept my mind active in [many] major book and video projects since terminal disease struck my life....

I long have felt that even if I am further restricted in my activities, I can go around the world for my Lord by interceding in prayer for others, especially for leaders.

Whether you have twenty years left, ten years, one year, one month, one day, or just one hour, there is something very important God wants you to do that can add to His kingdom and your blessing. He has called you to this hour. He has prepared you for this task. This is your destiny.

I am eighty-one and no longer in the fast lane. But Christians never retire from being servants of our great Creator-God and Savior. We are never too old to be in business with and for the King of kings. Feelings of uselessness and hopelessness are not from God, but from the evil one, the devil, who wants to discourage you and thwart your effectiveness for the Lord.

But, believe me, God wants to use you! Your life and mind are valuable to Him, and we all are still accountable to Him for how we spend our days.

Though I am in bed and on oxygen twenty-four hours each day, I am experiencing one of the most fruitful periods of my life. Whether or not you are mobile, there is even something greater you can do. Yes, I said greater!

Some readers might be able to do many other things, but there is one role any believer can aspire to: you can serve God in the high calling of a prayer intercessor! There is not a more important job in the body of Christ than that of an intercessor. Prayer intercession provides the power and foundation for everything else that is done, for the Lord God says, "Call to Me and I will answer you, and I will tell you great and mighty things, which you do not know" (Jer. 33:3 NASB).

> You can be a prayer intercessor while in a bed or a wheelchair. You can do it literally anywhere. If you do not have the strength to pray aloud, you can whisper it. If you cannot whisper, you can move your lips. If you cannot move your lips, then pray silently, in your mind. God knows and reads your heart. Remember what God says: "The earnest prayer of a righteous person has great power and wonderful results" (James 5:16). [13]

Bright's legacy ought to encourage us all to *continue on* – despite weakened bodies or even when facing the end. And, if the days come when we can do little physically, we can still engage in one of the most important works – persevering prayer.

The Example of the Apostle, Paul

Most commentators believe the apostle Paul wrote the book of 2 Timothy while he was in Rome awaiting trial and eventual execution. It was probably the last letter he wrote and in it, it is apparent that he is anticipating his impending death.

Probably more than any Bible character, Paul experienced hardship, persecution, and betrayal by friends. After becoming a Christian, he recounted five times receiving from his fellow countrymen thirty-nine lashes, three times beaten with rods, once stoned, three times shipwrecked, often without sleep, sometimes going without food, suffering physically from *a thorn in the flesh*, and being *exposed to death again and again.* [14] Now, in this final chapter of 2 Timothy, he mentions – in passing – a former friend, Demas, who had deserted him for the allurements of the world; Alexander, a metalworker who had done him much harm; and then during his first defense before the Romans, all his friends had forsaken him. [15]

Yet, as Paul is waiting in a dark and damp prison cell, with plenty of time to reflect over his life, there is no hint of resentment – either toward God or man. There is no bitterness detected in his spirit, nor any complaint of "unfairness." Neither is there a desire for escape, or wanting to experience some "deserved" relief and retirement. There is no sense of anxiety or gloominess as he awaits a likely end by execution. Rather, as an older man, Paul is full of faith and looking for the Lord! In the final chapter of his last book, he declared,

> *I have fought the good fight, I have finished the race, I have kept the faith. Now there is in store for me the crown of righteousness, which the Lord, the righteous Judge, will award to me on that day – and not only to me, but also to all who have longed for his appearing.*[16]

If you are facing the latter years of your life, what is your current attitude? Are you growing bitter because you have experienced neglect or even rejection by some family members? Are you anxious about your future finances? Are you fretting and complaining about physical discomforts?

Through the power of the Holy Spirit, you can have an optimistic and joyful faith like Paul had. Believe that God can help you also – not only to run your long-distance Christian "race," but to finish well! If this is your heart's desire, you can be assured you will have the help of heaven to accomplish it! Jesus Christ will make the difference in your life. *And I am sure that God, who began the good work within you, will continue his work until it is finally finished on that day when Christ Jesus comes back again.*[17]

CLOSING

A Personal Prayer As We Grow Older in the Grace of God

The greatest preparation we can make for old age and the age to come is to have an assurance of faith through a personal relationship with Jesus Christ.

I remember once talking to an elderly lady at a retirement home who was very sweet and a regular church-goer. In our conversation, however, I soon detected that she might not have a true Christian faith. So, I asked her a question I have used in sharing the message of Christ with many people.

> *Suppose you were to die today and stand at the gates of heaven. If you were greeted by an angel who asked you, "Why should you be allowed to enter heaven?" – what would be your response?*

She paused and then proceeded to tell me, "Well, I have tried to be a good person…" It was at this point, I realized how desperately she still needed assurance of salvation. As I shared with her the gospel – the good news about Christ – she understood and prayed with me.

How about you? Do you have a better answer than this? Are you depending upon your own good works or church attendance? If so, it is a shaky foundation for faith.

The Bible is Clear About Salvation

1. Jesus Christ came for people who know their need for God. He came not for those who think they are already "righteous," but for sinners.[18]

2. We must admit we are sinners. Every person born into the world is a sinner – that is, we all fall short

of pleasing God. We all break the commandments of God and tend to live a selfish life – basically doing our own thing in life.[19]

3. We must be willing to repent and be baptized. Repentance means that we will turn around from doing things *our* way and start doing things *God's* way. The outward action of baptism (immersion) is a testimony that we "die to ourselves" – no longer living for self, but for God's glory and the good of others.[20]

4. We must believe the biblical account – that Jesus Christ lived a perfect life on earth, died in our behalf, and rose again from the dead.[21]

5. We must make a verbal confession that "Jesus Christ is Lord of my Life." When we say "Lord," it means he is now the "Boss" man; the King who demands complete allegiance. He is now the #1 influence in the affairs of my life. This will affect my finances, my family, and the way I conduct business.[22]

6. We cannot depend on our own good works because we can never do enough. We must accept salvation as a wonderful *free* gift. We are saved simply by the grace of God through faith.[23]

7. As a new Christian we should seek to grow in our new faith. The Christian life is a *daily* walk with God. We grow by regularly reading God's word, talking to Him (prayer), assembling with other true believers, and sharing our faith with others.[24]

If you agree on these seven points, then you can read aloud this following prayer by faith for salvation. Such a prayer is never the end, but it can be the beginning of a wonderful journey of following Christ. We can be confident when we pray in the will of God, that he hears us.[25] If you pray such a prayer, please send me a note, so I can share your newfound joy!

PRAYER OF REPENTANCE

Heavenly Father, thank you I can come to you in Jesus' name. You have promised not to turn away *any* who come to you.

Thank you for your great love for me that sent Jesus to a terrible death on a cross to pay the price for my sins.

I recognize I am a sinner and in need of your salvation.

I realize all my good works fall short; I can do nothing to earn your favor. So, I receive the *free gift* of your salvation.

I ask your forgiveness of all my sins. Thank you that the shed blood of Jesus covers *all* my sins.

I repent and turn away from sin and a self-centered life. I now choose to follow God and do things his way.

I believe Jesus Christ died and rose again from the dead. I confess him as Lord of my life.

I ask you to become more real to me in the days ahead. Help me, personally, to know you better and understand your ways.

By the power of the Holy Spirit, help me to follow you the rest of my life. Help me to not only "run the race," but to finish well!

Thank you for your Son, Jesus Christ, and your great gift of salvation!

CHAPTER ONE NOTES: GROWING OLD IS NOT FOR SISSIES

Cartoon on p. 6 by Roz Chast, in *Last Laughs*, edited by Mort Gerberg (Simon and Schuster, NY, 2007)

[1] Adapted from three sources: Robert Morgan, *Nelson's Complete Book of Stories, Illustrations, and Quotes* (Thomas Nelson Publishers, Nashville, 2000) pp. 15-16; Gaynor McTique, *You Know You're Middle Age...* (Pinnacle books, 1994); and my own personal observations!

[2] From www.answers.com under "life expectancy" (Most of their information comes from *Encyclopedia Britannica.*) Also from *filipspagnoli.files.wordpress.com/2009/07life-expectancy* (research from Princeton Univ., Standford Univ., and World Health Organization.)

[3] See on web, *Pew Research Center Publications*, Dec. 20, 2010 article, "Baby Boomers Approach Age 65 – Glumly."

[4] Ps. 90:10

[5] Compare I Chr. 29:27-28 with II Sam. 5:4 and we see that David was seventy when he died.

[6] Ps. 92:14 NLT

[7] 1 Cor. 2:9

[8] Robert Browning, *Rabbi Ben Ezra* (1864)

[9] E. Stanley Jones, *Growing Spiritually* (Abington Press, Nashville, 1981)

CHAPTER TWO NOTES: KEEPING AN ETERNAL PERSPECTIVE

---

[1] 2 Cor. 4:16

[2] 1 Cor. 15:52-53 NLT

[3] Ecc. 12:1

[4] Ecc. 12:4-7 NLT

[5] Adapted from Art Linkletter, *Old Age is Not For Sissies* (Viking Penguin Group, NY, 1988) pp. 130-132

[6] Mark Buchanan, *Things Unseen* (Multonomah Publishers, Sisters, OR, 2002), p.180

[7] Rom. 12:2; Ps. 27:13 NAS

[8] Ps. 90:1-2, 9-12

[9] Jn. 10:10

[10] Jn. 1:4

[11] 1 Jn. 5:12

[12] C. S. Lewis, The Business of Heaven, (Mariner Books, NY, 1984) Mar. 4 devotional.

[13] Jerry Bridges, who worked under Trotman in the Navigators, recalled that statement. See John Piper and Justin Taylor, *Stand* (Crossway Books, Wheaton, Il, 2008) p. 87

[14] Betty Malz, *My Glimpse of Eternity* (Revell, Old Tappan, NJ, 1983)

[15] James Dobson, *Focus on the Family Newsletter* (Colorado Springs, CO), Oct. 2002

[16] Mk. 8:36 says, "What good is it for a man to gain the whole world, yet forfeit his soul?"

[17] Matt. 6:33

[18] Frances Havergal, quoted in Mary Tileston, *Daily Strength for Daily Needs* (Whitaker House, Springdale, PA, 1997)

[19] Oswald Sanders, *Earthen Vessels* (Discovery House Publishers, Grand Rapids, MI, 2005), p.182

[20] Horatius Bonar, *The Night of Weeping, Or, Words For the Suffering Family of God* (Kessinger Publishers, Whitefish, MT, 1849, 2010) p. 175

[21] 1 Cor. 3:10-14

[22] Joni Eareckson Tada, *Pearls of Great Price,* (Zondervan, Grand Rapids, MI, 2005) Mar. 30 devotional

CHAPTER THREE NOTES: BATTLING THE BEAUTY MYTH

---

[1] Statistical information comes from Naomi Wolf *The Beauty Myth* (Harper-Collins, NY, 2002) and the American Society of Plastic Surgeons (www.plasticsurgery.org)

[2] 2 Tim. 3:1-4

[3] Gen. 1:31

[4] Gen. 12:11

[5] Gen. 24:16

[6] Gen. 29:17

[7] Est. 2:7

[8] 1 Sam. 25:3

[9] Hebrew. sekel in *The Brown-Driver-Briggs Hebrew and English Lexicon* (Hendrickson Publishers, Peabody, MA. Originally published 1906)

[10] Gen. 1:10

[11] William Wilson, *Wilson's Old Testament Word Studies* (Hendrickson Publishers, Peabody, MA, 1993)

[12] Matt. 6:22 Contemporary English Version

[13] Matt. 23:27

[14] 1 Pet. 3:3-5 NLT

[15] Prov. 31:30

[16] Abraham Lincoln, December 23, 1863, as he related to John Hay, in John Barlett, *Bartlett's Familiar Quotations* (Little, Brown, and Co., Boston, 1866, 1980) p. 523

[17] Is. 53:2
[18] Ezek. 28:12
[19] Ezek. 28:17
[20] Prov. 15:13
[21] Bill Gothard, booklet *Self Acceptance* (Institute in Basic Youth Conflicts, Oak Brook, Il) pp. 15-16
[22] Ibid., p.8
[23] 1 Cor. 15:42-53 NLT

CHAPTER FOUR NOTES: CLEANING OUT THE CLUTTER

---

[1] 1 Cor. 14:33
[2] 1 Cor. 14:40 NAS with Greek translations in brackets
[3] Col. 2:5 RSV
[4] Joseph Thayer, *Thayer's Greek-English Lexicon of the New Testament* (Associated Publishers, Grand Rapids, MI)
[5] Macon Rich, a member of my church, has such a business/ministry – check out web: caringsolutions.info.; or contact Macon by email at macon.rich@yahoo.com Macon also recommends two organizations found in many communities: Certified Senior Advisors and National Association of Senior Move Managers.
[6] Phil. 4:13

CHAPTER FIVE NOTES: CARING FOR ELDERLY RELATIVES

---

[1] Jn. 19:26-27
[2] A. T. Robertson, *Word Pictures in the New Testament, Vol. IV* (Baker Book House, Grand Rapids, MI, 1931) pp. 583-584
[3] William Hendricksen, *New Testament Commentary: Thessalonians, Timothy, and Titus* (Baker Book House, Grand Rapids, MI, 1979) p. 169
[4] *The Practical Works of Richard Baxter, Vol. 1*, (Soli Deo Gloria Publishers, Ligonier, PA, 1990), p. 454
[5] Charles Swindoll, *Swindoll's New Testament Insights on 1 & 2 Timothy, Titus* ((Zondervan, Grand Rapids, MI, 2010) p. 101
[6] Rev. 12:10
[7] Rom. 8:1 emphasis mine
[8] Rom. 14:22 NLT
[9] From Website, *Power to Change*, iTV Network (Langley, B.C. Canada)
[10] Ed Wheat, *Love Life For Every Married Couple* (Zondervan, Grand Rapids, MI, 1980) pp. 120-121
[11] Eph. 4:2 The Amplified Bible
[12] 1 Pet. 4:8
[13] Billy Graham, online interview with *Christianity Today,* January 2011.
[14] Source unknown

CHAPTER SIX NOTES: WATCHING OVER WIDOWS

[1] Prov. 14:10 NLT
[2] Vance Havner, *Though I Walk Through the Valley* (Fleming Revell, Old Tappan, NJ, 1974) pp. 91, 121
[3] Adapted from Lauren Briggs, *What to Say When You Don't Know What to Say,* (Harvest House Publishers, Eugene, OR), pp. 150-155
[4] Spiro Zodhiates, The Complete Word Study Bible and Dictionary (AMG Publishers, Chattanooga, TN, 1992)
[5] Matt. 25:36
[6] Eph. 2:19 The Living Bible
[7] Ex. 22:22-24
[8] Deut. 27:19
[9] Is. 1:17
[10] Mk. 12:41-44
[11] Lk. 7:11-17
[12] Jn. 19:25-27
[13] 1 Tim. 5:3-16
[14] John MacArthur, online message, "Widows in the Church – Part One." See www.gty.org
[15] Alexander Strauch, *The New Testament Deacon* (Lewis and Roth Publishers, Littleton, CO, 1992) p. 156
[16] 1 Pet. 4:8-9
[17] Ps. 68:6

CHAPTER SEVEN NOTES: EMBRACING GOD'S BEST PROMISES FOR OLD AGE

[1] 2 Pet. 1:4
[2] Billy Graham, *The Journey* (W Publishing Group, Nashville, 2006) p. 294
[3] Deut. 1:31
[4] Ps. 55:22 NAS
[5] Ps. 27:10 NKJV
[6] Ps. 46:1
[7] Ps. 31:15
[8] *Journal and Letters of Henry Martyn* (Protestant Episcopal Society for the Promotion of Evangelical Knowledge, 1851) p. 460
[9] Ps. 118:17
[10] Roger Martin, *Apostle of Certainty* (Sword of the Lord Publishers, Murfreesboro, TN, 2000) pp. 254-255
[11] Ibid.

[12] This thought comes from John Phillips, *Exploring Here and There, Vol.II* (Ambassador-Emerald International, Greenville, SC, 2000) p. 69
[13] Heb. 13:5 NKJV
[14] Matt. 28:20
[15] Phillip Keller, *A Shepherd Looks at the 23rd Psalm* (Zondervan, Grand Rapids, MI, 2008) p. 44
[16] Spiro Zodhiates, *The Complete Word Study Bible and Dictionary* (AMG Publishers, Chattanooga, TN, 1992)
[17] Ibid.,
[18] Rev. 22:13
[19] Phil. 2:13
[20] Eph. 2:10 Greek
[21] Ps. 23:6 NLT
[22] Rom. 2:4 NKJV
[23] Ps. 27:13 NAS
[24] Ps. 136:1

CHAPTER EIGHT NOTES: MAINTAINING A JOYFUL AND GRATEFUL HEART

---

[1] Don Colbert, interview in *Charisma* magazine (Lake Mary, FL), Oct. 2004 issue.
[2] Stanley C. Baldwin, *A Funny Thing Happened on My Way to Old Age* (InterVarsity Press, Downers Grove, Il, 2005) p. 24
[3] Phil. 2:14 NAS
[4] Graham Miller, *Calvin's Wisdom* (The Banner of Truth Trust, Carlisle, PA, 1992), p. 229
[5] Hannah Whitall Smith, *The God of All Comfort* (James Nisbet and Co., London, 1906) p. 203
[6] I Thes. 5:16,18
[7] Judson Cornwall, *Dying With Grace* (Charisma House, Lake Mary, Fl., 2004) p. xi.
[8] Article, "Author Judson Cornwall Dies" by Eric Tiansay, *Charisma* magazine (charismamag.com), written March 31, 2005
[9] Cornwall, *Dying With Grace,* p. 46
[10] 1 Thes. 5:16-18
[11] Neh. 8:10
[12] Rom. 14:17
[13] Jn. 15:5-7
[14] Ps. 127:1
[15] Matt. 11:28-29
[16] Zech. 4:6
[17] Robert Peterson and Alexander Strauch, *Agape Leadership* (Lewis and Roth Publishers, Littleton, CO, 1991) pp. 65-66

[18] Tim Hansel, *You Gotta Keep Dancin'; In the Midst of Life's Hurts You Can Choose Joy* (David C. Cook Publishing Co., Elgin, Il, 1985), p. 55
[19] Phil. 4:11
[20] Billy Graham, online interview with *Christianity Today,* January 2011.
[21] Elisabeth Elliot Gren newsletter (Magnolia, MA), March 2003

CHAPTER NINE NOTES: FACING DEATH WITH AN OPTIMISTIC FAITH

---

[1] C. S. Lewis, *The Weight of Glory and Other Addresses* (MacMillan, NY, 1939, revised 1980) pp. 21-22
[2] Heb. 9:27 NKJV
[3] Ecc. 9:12
[4] Rom. 14:7-9
[5] Rom. 14:8-9 Phillips
[6] Jn. 11:25
[7] Phil. 1:21 Phillips
[8] Derek Prince Newsletter (Charlotte, NC), March 1999
[9] Robert J. Morgan, *On This Day* (Nelson, Nashville, 1997) August 3 devotional.
[10] Job 14:14
[11] Roy Zuck, commentary on Job, in *The Bible Knowledge Commentary*, edited by John Walvoord and Roy Zuck (Victor Books, Wheaton, IL, 1985) p. 736
[12] Dick Bohrer, paraphrase edition, *John Newton: Letters of a Slave Trader Freed By God's Grace* (Moody Press, Chicago, 1983) p. 120
[13] Phil. 1:23-24
[14] William Barclay, *The Letters to the Philippians, Colossians, and Thessalonians* (The Westminster Press, Philadelphia, 1975) p. 28
[15] *The Apology of Aristides the Philosopher,* Section XV, translated by D. M. Kay, University of Edinburgh. See www.earlychristian writings.com/ text/aristides-kay.html
[16] Told by Billy Graham in the article, "Death is a Transition," *Decision* magazine (Charlotte, NC) Sept. 2002 issue.
[17] Heb. 11:13-16
[18] Thomas Watson, *Gleanings from Thomas Watson* (Soli Deo Gloria Publications, Morgan, PA, 1995) p. 115
[19] Ps. 118:17
[20] Ps. 31:9-15 emphasis mine
[21] John Pollock, *A Fistful of Heroes* (Christian Focus Publications, Great Britain, 1998) p. 104
[22] James Snyder, *In Pursuit of God: The Life of A. W. Tozer* (Christian Publications, Camp Hill, PA, 1991) p. 46
[23] Charles Spurgeon, sermon entitled "Precious Deaths," on Feb. 18, 1872, See *Spurgeon's Expository Encyclopedia,* (Baker Book House, Grand Rapids, MI, 1996) Vol. 6, p. 162

[24] Acts 13:36
[25] 1 Cor. 15:52-53
[26] Matt. 25:21
[27] John Pollock, *Moody* (Zondervan Publishing House, Grand Rapids, MI, 1963) p. 316
[28] 2 Cor. 5:6-8
[29] 1 Jn. 3:2-3
[30] Ps. 17:15 TLB
[31] Mark Water, compiler, *The New Encyclopedia of Christian Quotations* (Baker Books, Grand Rapids, MI, 2000) p. 254
[32] *Our Daily Bread* (Radio Bible Class, Grand Rapids, MI) Feb. 2001 issue
[33] 1 Cor. 15:26
[34] Heb. 2:14-15 NLT
[35] Mrs. Howard Taylor, *The Triumph of John and Betty Stam* (China Inland Mission, Philadelphia, 1935) pp. 104-105

CHAPTER TEN NOTES: LEAVING A LASTING LEGACY

---

[1] *Webster's New Universal Unabridged Dictionary* (Random House Value Publishers, NY, 1996)
[2] Prov. 13:22
[3] Is. 38:1
[4] Num. 27:8-11
[5] Ecc. 7:11-12 NKJV
[6] Mark Water, compiler, *The New Encyclopedia of Christian Quotations* (Baker Books, Grand Rapids, MI, 2000, pp. 587-594
[7] Charles Colson, *The Good Life* (Tyndale House Publishers, Wheaton, Il, 2005) pp. 138-140
[8] Article by John McElroy, "Leaving a Legacy," found on website of "Ministries of Francis Frangipane." McElroy has also written a book on this subject, *Passing the Baton.*
[9] 2 Tim. 1:5
[10] *The New Encyclopedia of Christian Quotations,* p. 531
[11] 1 Pet. 1:4

CHAPTER ELEVEN NOTES: RESISTING THE RETIREMENT MENTALITY

---

[1] Lk. 12:19

[2] John Piper, message "Getting Old to the Glory of God." From website, www.desiringgod.org 2007 National Conference Messages, p. 48

[3] Article by Kelly Stern, Age with Vitality," in *Kindred Spirit*, Spring/Summer 2011, Vol. 35, No. 1 (Dallas Theological Seminary, Dallas, TX)

[4] Num. 13 and 14

[5] Josh. 14:10-12 NKJV

[6] Lk. 2:36-38

[7] Charles Colson, *The Body* (Word Publishing, Dallas, 1992) pp. 332-3

[8] W. M. Douglas, *Andrew Murray and His Message* (Baker Book House, Grand Rapids, MI, 1981) p. 256

[9] Ibid., p. 238

[10] The Works of John Wesley, Vol. 4 (Baker Book House, Grand Rapids, MI, 1996) p. 427

[11] John T. and Ruth Seamands, *Engineered for Glory: The Story of E. A. Seamands* (Francis Asbury Society, Wilmore, KY) p. 159

[12] Ibid., p. 116

[13] Paul Tournier, *Learn To Grow Old* (Harper and Row Publishers, NY, 1971) pp. 20-21

[14] Charles Colson, *The Good Life* (Tyndale House Publishers, Wheaton, Il, 2005) p. 87

[15] Article by Stacey Hamby, "96 Too Young to Retire," published originally by Baptist Press, late in *Pulpit Helps* (Chattanooga, TN) Feb. 2001 issue.

[16] Harry Verploegh, *Oswald Chambers: The Best From All His Works* (Thomas Nelson Publishers, Nashville, 1987) p. 47

[17] Tit. 2:12 Phillips

[18] John Ortberg, *God is Closer Than You Think* (Zondervan Publishing House, Grand Rapids, 2005) p. 67

[19] Story told by Charles Swindoll, *The Quest For Character* (Multnomah Press, Portland, OR, 1987) pp. 205-206

[20] Charles Swindoll, in *Christianity Today* interview on CT Website www.christianitytoday.com 4/15/2010

[21] Personal notes from Bo Barredo (Advancing Native Missions, Charlottesville, VA)

[22] E. Stanley Jones, *Christian Maturity* (Abingdon Press, Nashville, TN, 1991)

[23] E. Stanley Jones, *A Song of Ascents* (Abingdon Press, Nashville, TN, 1968), p. 20

CHAPTER TWELVE NOTES: FINISHING OUR RACE WELL

---

[1] Ecc. 7:8
[2] Phil. 3:10-14
[3] Heb. 12:1-2
[4] 1 Cor. 9:25-27
[5] Heb. 12:1
[6] Matt. 10:22
[7] Lk. 8:15
[8] Cited in Howard Dayton, *Your Money Map* (Moody Publishers, Chicago, 2006) p. 240
[9] Paul D. Stanley and J. Robert Clinton, *Connecting* (NavPress, Colorado Springs, CO, 1992) p. 215
[10] 1 Sam. 8:1
[11] 1 Sam. 12:23-24
[12] V. Raymond Edman, *The Disciplines of Life* (World Wide Publications, Minneapolis, 1948) p. 51
[13] Bill Bright, *The Journey Home* (Guideposts, Carmel, NY, 2003) pp. 103-105 (my emphasis added in italics)
[14] 2 Cor. 11:23-12:10
[15] 2 Tim. 4:10-18
[16] 2 Tim. 4:7-8
[17] Phil. 1:6
[18] Matt. 5:3; Lk. 19:10
[19] Is. 53:6; Rom. 3:23; 6:23
[20] Mk. 1:15; Lk. 15:7; Acts 2:38-39; Rom. 6:4-6
[21] 1 Cor. 15:3-4; Rom. 10:9-10
[22] Rom. 10:9-10; Lk. 6:46
[23] Eph. 2:8-9; Rom. 6:23
[24] 1 Pet. 2:2: Lk. 9:23; John 8:31-32; Heb. 10:25
[25] 1 John 5:11-15